Healing
the Jesus Way

Don Double

with Tim Jones

D1628228

New Wine Press

Other books by Don Double

Life in a new dimension
Live like a king
The five facts of life
It's the greatest day you ever lived
The positive power of the fear of God
What to do in a storm
Victory over Depression

Also

It's a wonderful new life
Don Double's biography
by Eileen Thompson

ISBN 0 947852 867

Typeset by CRB Typesetting Services, Ely, Cambs.
Printed by Richard Clay Ltd, Bungay Suffolk.

Contents

Acknowledgements

Thanks are due to a number of people who were involved in the preparation of this book:

to Anne Double and Faith Double for typing the text onto the computer,

to Mike Darwood and Jonathan Conrathe for their helpful comments and advice,

and to Heather Double for her help and support.

This book is dedicated to all those who are sick
or suffering in any way and are willing
to look to Jesus for their healing.

Throughout the book you will find 'Healing Highlights.' These are all testimonies of people who have been healed through the ministry of Don Double and the Good News Crusade team. They are not included to bring glory to Don and the team, the glory for these healings belongs to the Lord Jesus Christ.

Most of the people who are mentioned were healed some time ago. This is to show that when God heals someone, His desire is to bring permanent release. Don't believe for temporary relief and expect a relapse a few months or years later.

These testimonies are evidence of what God can do. We pray that they will encourage your faith. It may be that you are sick, and suffer from a similar complaint as one of the people included. Know that these people are not 'special,' they suffered in the same way as you do, they know what the pain feels like. But also know that they made contact with God, and they experienced healing – **The Jesus Way**. You can too.

Chapter 1

Healing the Jesus Way – I

Jesus is a Healer. Even a quick reading of the Gospels reveals that Jesus healed people. He healed them in a variety of ways, but it is important to realise that He always healed those that came to Him. I cannot find anywhere in the Bible where Jesus ever refused to heal anyone. The Gospels are clear about this, and then in the book of Acts, you will find that He just continued doing the same thing through the early Church. There is no record in the Word of God where Jesus ever refused to heal anyone. Be encouraged by that. Whoever you are, whatever your condition, know that Jesus does not refuse to heal people.

The Bible says in Hebrews 13:8, *'Jesus Christ is the same yesterday, today, and forever.'* Jesus has not changed, has he? No. I want you to get hold of that fact as we look at the many ways Jesus used to heal people.

Jesus is the kind of person who came against religion. As you read the Gospels, you will find that Jesus' battles were never with sinners, publicans, adulterers, or prostitutes. He never had problems with those kind of folk. The people that Jesus clashed with were the religious leaders and authorities. He never allowed them to put His healing power into a little box or tell Him how or when to heal a sick person. We must make sure that we don't try to do that to Jesus, today. Jesus loved variety and as you read the Gospels you will find there are so many different ways He used to heal the people He met.

What I want us to do at the beginning of this book is to look at some of the ways Jesus used to heal people.

1. The Touch – Part I

The first one we will look at is the people Jesus touched. There is a chorus we used to sing on our crusades, that expresses something of what the people Jesus touched must have felt:

'He touched me, Oh He touched me
And Oh the joy that floods my soul,
Something happened, and now I know
He touched me and made me whole.'

And the good news is that Jesus still goes about touching people; perhaps He will come to where you are sitting and touch you as you read this book. You have my permission to get excited, to jump out of your seat and start shouting Hallelujah, if He touches you! That often happens in my meetings; I remember a man who came into a meeting, blind in one eye and almost blind in the other. I was preaching the gospel and in the middle of my sermon he began to shout out at the top his voice, 'I can see! I can see!' He had been completely healed because Jesus had touched him.

In the eighth chapter of Matthew a leper asks Jesus to heal him. *'Jesus put out His hand and touched him, saying "I am willing, be cleansed."'* Immediately, the leprosy left his body and he was clean. (Matthew 8:3). This man knew that Jesus could heal him, but he doubted if it really was God's will. Jesus touched him and proved what God's will is.

'And He touched her hand, and the fever left her. Then she arose and served them.' (Matthew 8:15) After preaching at the synagogue in Capernaum, Jesus went to Peter's home. There they found Peter's mother-in-law sick; when Jesus touched her, the fever went, she got up and helped get them lunch.

'Then He touched their eyes, saying "According to your faith let it be to you."' (Matthew 9:29) Jesus touched many blind eyes and opened them. Bringing sight to blind eyes was a

10

frequent occurrence in Jesus' ministry. In fact when John the Baptist's disciples came to ask if He was the Messiah, Jesus pointed to blind people seeing as one of the proofs He was who He said He was. (Luke 7).

'But Jesus answered and said, "Permit even this." And He touched his ear and healed him.' (Luke 22:51). The man was deaf and He touched his ear and he could hear. Under the anointing of the Holy Spirit, I have touched many deaf ears and they have been opened.

I believe one of the ways God touches people today is through the Word of Knowledge. (1 Corinthians 12:8). Through the Holy Spirit, God comes and touches us; what God is saying through the word of knowledge is 'Hey! I know you are here, and I know what your condition is. Know that I love you. I am sending my healing power into your body, believe it, receive it, reach out with your faith and receive what I am sending you.'

The Lord regularly speaks to people this way in my meetings; one instance will illustrate what I am saying. I was in a meeting in London and as we were ministering I had a word of knowledge. It was for a woman who had a condition in her body that her G.P. had not been able to diagnose. Obviously this was worrying her, to the extent that she was full of anxiety. God also showed me that the G.P. had arranged for her to visit a Consultant on the following Friday afternoon. The moment I said that, a lady started to walk down the aisle, tears streaming down her face. I laid my hands on her head, touching her in the name of Jesus and as I did she fell to the floor as the power of God started to work in her body. She lay there for quite a while. When she got up the Glory of God was clearly all over her face and I believe that the Lord had completely healed her. That's God touching you; He knows the date of your appointment for the specialist and all those other details.

'And He took him aside from the multitude, and put His fingers in his ears, and He spat and touched his tongue.' (Mark 7:33) At times Jesus did things that are very unconventional. Putting your finger in someone's ear might seem strange to

11

you and I don't know whether you would like this particular way, but this is a 'Jesus way.' As British people we would probably say that was a bit crude, but crude or not, the man was healed. As his ears were opened, his tongue was loosed and he could speak.

In a crusade in Zimbabwe five deaf mutes were brought to our meeting and we prayed for them in the Name of Jesus. We did not spit on them nor did we touch their tongues, no word came to do that, but I would if God had told me to. As we prayed God opened their ears and those boys could hear for the first time in their lives. Obviously they needed to be taught to speak so we began right there. Their first words were 'Jesus,' and my name, 'Don.'

2. The Touch – Part II

I want you to understand that there is a big difference between Jesus touching **you** and you touching **Jesus**. By an act of your will and using your faith, you can touch Jesus. **You can touch Jesus.** How can you touch Jesus? In Matthew 28:20 Jesus promises you that *'I am with you always, even to the end of the age.'* You can't see Him with your physical eyes, but He has said He will be with us. You can reach out and touch him.

In Mark chapter 5 we read of a woman who had been sick for twelve years. Despite the crowds around Jesus she pushed through and came up behind Him. She said within herself *'If only I may touch His clothes, I shall be made well.'* (Mark 5:28). The moment she touched the hem of his garment, she was healed. The exciting thing for me about this story, is that the moment she touched Jesus, He knew something had happened. In the King James version, it says, *'Virtue went out of Him.'* Virtue in this context is power, healing power. Let me tell everybody who is sick and reading this book – your greatest need is to touch Jesus with the kind of touch that will cause the virtue to leave Jesus and come into you. The only thing that can heal you is the power of Jesus working in you.

I have been in meetings where thousands of people

responded; on one occasion over 10,000 people responded to Jesus for healing. Obviously, it is impossible to lay hands on that many people and so each person has to use their faith. As we began to minister to the sick in Jesus name, we told them to reach out to Jesus, just as the woman with the issue of blood had. Hundreds of people in the crowd did as we told them, but not all were healed. Why? Only some people touched Jesus with faith and as they did, virtue left Jesus and came into them and they were healed. It was their faith that made the difference. I tell you the truth, if you touch Jesus with that kind of faith, virtue will leave Him and come into you. You see, the woman had settled in her heart that she would be healed; as she touched the hem of His garment she **was** going to be healed.

One of the issues we need to face is the question of timing. 'It's not God's time for me,' should never be used as an excuse for not being healed. You cannot find a 'guaranteed' method that will produce a result every time; there is no 'normal' way to be healed. Jesus chooses the way and the time He will heal you. But because we are not healed it is no good saying it wasn't God's time. I believe the issue in touching Jesus is that we get through to Jesus.

It's no good coming to Don Double, or any other man, with the idea that we are special people who can lay hands on everybody and heal folk. If I could heal at will, on a whim or a fancy, I know I would go and heal everybody I could get my hands on, because that's the way I feel. I believe that's the way Jesus feels too, the Gospels make it clear that Jesus was filled with compassion for the sick people He met. But you have got to get through to Him, that is the key to being healed.

The more I travel the world and the more miracles I see, I have come to accept one fundamental truth. God is sovereign and He chooses the way and the time for a person's healing. I strongly believe that we have a responsibility to seek God, use our faith and believe His will for us, but there is a 'divine tension,' between that and God's sovereignty. We must seek God and ask, but He choses the time and the place.

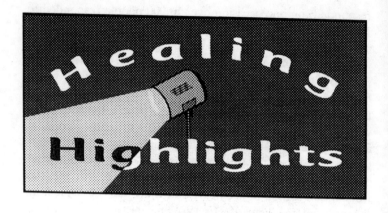

Elizabeth Nakanwagi

Elizabeth is Ugandan and lives in the capital city, Kampala. In 1987 she could not walk; she could only get about either by struggling on crutches or by being carried on a stretcher.

In October 1987 Don held his first Good News Crusade in the city, in a sports stadium. Some friends carried Elizabeth to the crusade hoping that she might be prayed for, because her doctor had said she had only days to live. There were many things wrong with her and the team learnt later that the doctors suspected that she had the AIDS virus.

When holding overseas crusades, the numbers of people wanting prayer for healing is often too great to pray for everyone individually. Don usually asks the people to stand and put their hand on the place that needs healing. He then prays a general prayer believing that the Holy Spirit will move across the crowd touching everyone that wants to be healed. Don then invites the people who have been healed to come forward and testify from the platform to what God has done for them.

After praying in this way, Elizabeth was able to walk, with some assistance, to the platform and glorified Jesus, saying that something had happened.

Elizabeth met Don again in February 1990, during his second crusade in Kampala, and Don reports that she is perfectly well. She is walking with no pain and is enjoying a healthy life.

*Elizabeth came to the platform to
testify what God had done for her.
It was at first a struggle but she
passed her crutches to the brother on
the left and walked unaided to Don.*

Healing or the Healer?

The truth is you can go to heaven with a sick body but you will never get there with a sin sick soul. The first important step is to get to *know* Jesus, to know Him as your personal saviour, Lord and friend. Then you will know Him as your healer.

'Whenever He entered, into villages, cities, or the country, they laid the sick in the marketplaces, and begged Him that they might just touch the border of His garment. And as many as touched Him were made well.' (Mark 6:56). **As many as touched Him** – that's what the Bible says. *'Jesus Christ, is the same yesterday, today and forever'* (Heb 13:8). Therefore we can believe the same is true for us. When we settle in our hearts that it is God's time, when we touch Him in faith, we will experience His healing power. Luke 6:19 records that *'the whole multitude sought to touch Him, for power went out from Him and healed them all.'* If you reach out with that kind of faith, you will be healed.

3. The Touch – Part III: The Laying on of Hands

'Now when the sun was setting, all those who had anyone sick with various diseases brought them to Him; and He laid His hands on every one of them and healed them.' (Luke 4:40). In Mark 16:18 it says *'they will lay hands on the sick, and they will recover,'* Hallelujah! Laying on of hands is another method of being healed. I will lay hands on anyone who wants hands laid on them. When we lay hands on the sick we are doing what God's Word says and we expect the results that Jesus said were going to happen – recovery. Because God's word says it I believe He will do what He said He will do. *'They shall lay hands on the sick and they **will** recover.'* Not *might* do, not *could* do, not there is a possibility that it will happen, He said **will**. I am going to believe **will**. If everybody I laid hands on died, I would still believe **will**, because His word says it (and by the way, most people I lay hands on recover).

4. The Spoken Word

'I did not even think myself worthy to come to You. But say the word, and my servant will be healed.' (Luke 7:7). We can be healed by the power of God's spoken word. In Luke 7 we read about the Roman Centurion, who comes to Jesus for his sick servant. As the centurion knew, there are times when all you need is the Word. There is a moment when you hear the Word of God, and can say 'That's for me. That's a gift from God, I know it's mine.' As God sends His Word, be assured that the Bible says that heaven and earth can pass away but the Word of God will never pass away. (Matthew 24:35). God will watch over that special Word until it happens and accomplishes all that it was sent for. Why? The Word is impregnated with life. At the moment it gets into you, you become 'pregnant' with a miracle. That's what happens when His healing word comes to you.

5. Obedience

*'Now as Jesus passed by, He saw a man who was blind from birth. And His disciples asked Him, saying, "Rabbi, who sinned, this man or his parents, that he was born blind?" Jesus answered, "Neither this man nor his parents sinned, but that the works of God should be revealed in him. I must work the works of Him who sent Me while it is day; **the** night is coming when no one can work. As long as I am in the world, I am the light of the world." When He had said these things, He spat on the ground and made clay with the saliva; and He anointed the eyes of the blind man with the clay. And He said to him, "Go, wash in the pool of Siloam" (which is translated, Sent). So he went and washed, and came back seeing.'*   (John 9:1–7).

What an unusual way for somebody to be healed. Standing before Jesus is a man blind from birth. First Jesus spat on the ground (just doing that alone would upset most people) but then he rubbed the dust into his saliva and then smeared it onto the man's eyes. It was probably as well that the man was blind and couldn't see what Jesus was doing!

If you saw someone do this I am sure you'd think that it would make things worse. Very often when I pray for people to be healed, the first thing they feel is worse. In some of the greatest miracles that have happened, the first sign was that the person felt worse. I can't explain it, I am not the healer. One day when we get to heaven we will have time just to talk to Jesus, and ask him why He did things the way He did.

I have heard all sorts of explanations about why Jesus healed this man in the way he did. Some of them seem valid but all I want to stress is that this man obeyed God. He did what he was told and went down to the pool of Siloam and washed. It was ordinary water, with nothing special about it, but when he washed the clay off his eyes, he could see.

Whatever God says to you do it. When it comes to obedience it's easy – either we do or we don't obey. On one occasion, I was preaching from the account in Luke 17 of the ten lepers. Jesus told them to, *'Go, show yourselves to the priests.'* No prayer, just a simple command. After my meeting had finished, a man came forward for healing. I did the same as Jesus and simply said, 'Go home, right now in Jesus Name.' He went obediently and God touched him. You have to obey. I don't know what God might say to you, but whatever He says you must do it.

In this chapter we've seen how Jesus touched people and how they touched him, how He spoke a Word that healed, and how obedience will produce healing. I hope that you are beginning to realise that healing is not something that God dangles just out of our reach, like the donkey and the carrot. God is a good God and we need to begin believing that fact. The faith God has given for us to use can have an important affect on whether we are healed or not. In the next chapter we will look at some more of the ways Jesus healed and how our faith does affect the outcome.

Chapter 2

Healing the Jesus Way – II

As we saw in the first chapter Jesus healed many people and for each of them He knew exactly the right way to meet their need. Let's look at some more ways:

6. Faith

> *'Again He entered Capernaum after some days, and it was heard that He was in the house. Immediately many gathered together, so that there was no longer room to receive them, not even near the door. And He preached the word to them. Then they came to Him, bringing a paralytic who was carried by four men. And when they could not come near Him because of the crowd, they uncovered the roof where He was. And when they had broken through, they let down the bed on which the paralytic was lying. When Jesus saw their faith, He said to the paralytic, "Son, your sins are forgiven you."'* (Mark 2:1–5).

Verse five says that Jesus saw their faith. Jesus saw their faith and he healed the man. You can see faith. Faith is tangible. Some people get the idea that faith is a 'Pie in the sky' type of thing, something for dreamers which doesn't have much reality in it. I want to tell you that faith is not 'pie in the sky if you die,' it's 'steak on the plate while you wait!' It's something you can have right now, Hallelujah! You can see faith.

You can usually tell when people have faith. Sometimes as I stand before lines of people, who have come for prayer, I just look down the line and I can see those who have faith. For them it's easy to say, 'Be healed in Jesus Name.'

7. Deliverance

This is one area where faith is very necessary. We must not be afraid of the reality of demons or devils. What God did through Jesus on the Cross defeated the devil. Satan was completely defeated at the Cross. When demons are responsible for sickness in people's bodies, the first thing we need to declare is that on the cross Jesus dealt an eternal death blow to Satan. If we are repentant and washed in the blood of Jesus, he has no legal right to stay in our lives any more. It is important to ensure that there are no landing strips for him to come back to.

What do I mean by landing strips? In Africa and many third world countries the only place an airplane can set down is a strip of land that has been cleared of rocks and shrubs. I've landed on strips where the goats and sheep have been shooed off just before the plane landed! Usually the landing strip has to be flat enough to ensure that the plane doesn't 'flip' over as it lands or takes off. One way of stopping the plane using a strip is to plough it up and make it too rough for use. How does that apply in our lives? Satan can use areas of unconfessed sin to land and bring sickness and trouble into our lives.

A graphic illustration of this is the many times in our meetings that people have forgiven someone of a long held grudge. They come crippled by arthritis or rheumatism and as they speak the words of forgiveness they are also healed. By nursing a hurt or disappointment, they provided an area in their lives for Satan to land and get to work with his destructive powers. By repenting and confessing those sins, the landing strips are 'ploughed' up and Satan has to leave.

'Now He was teaching in one of the synagogues on the Sabbath. And behold, there was a woman who had a spirit

*of infirmity eighteen years, and was bent over and could in
no way raise herself up. But when Jesus saw her, He called
her to Him and said to her, "Woman, you are loosed from
your infirmity."'* (Luke 13:10–12).

The Bible says the woman had a spirit of infirmity and it was
in her back, she was bent double looking down at her toes. I
believe the probable diagnosis today would be that she had an
arthritic spine. She had been like it for 18 years, but as Jesus
told the spirit to go, she stood up straight, completely free
from the demon. I've seen the same thing happen many times
in our meetings.

*'But if I cast out demons by the Spirit of God, surely the
kingdom of God has come upon you.'* (Matthew 12:28). When
demon powers are cast out in Jesus name, the Kingdom of
God is come to us. The name of Jesus is not a magic formula
like 'Abracadabra.' His is the name that is above every other
Name. *'At the name of Jesus every knee should bow, of those in
heaven, and of those on earth, and of those under the earth, and
that every tongue should confess that Jesus Christ is Lord, to the
glory of God the Father.'* (Philippians 2:10–11).

Every knee must bow in submission to Jesus, the King of
Kings. All the demons and devils and evil spirits must obey
commands made in the name of Jesus, because Jesus is Lord
of Lords. As Jesus' healing power is seen, His Kingdom is
established, Hallelujah!

8. Anointing with Oil

*'And they cast out many demons, and anointed with oil many
who were sick, and healed them.'* (Mark 6:13). When the
disciples were sent out two by two to preach the Gospel, they
anointed people with oil. In His instructions before they went
Jesus does not mention this but it seems to be accepted as a
valid means. Later in James 5:14 anointing with oil by the
elders is used for healing. It is yet another way and one we can
use.

Carol Griffiths

Carol's doctor had told her that the pain she suffered was caused by a degeneration of her spine. Instead of having a straight spine it was splitting in two. This was confirmed by X-rays and it was obviously a source of great pain.

After responding at one of Don's meetings, Don prayed for Carol. She 'went out,' collapsing and falling to the floor as the Holy Spirit touched her and began to heal her. Afterwards Carol said that as she lay on the floor she felt the Lord touch her, a few inches above where the X-ray showed the problem to be. She says 'I had a complete overhaul and all the pain has gone.'

Smith Wigglesworth, that great apostle of faith, filled auditoriums around Britain with people wanting to see his healing ministry. On one occasion he was sick and every method of healing had failed; people had prayed for him, they had fasted, they tried to get anyone who had a healing ministry to pray for him. They tried everything and still he did not get healed. One day as he read the scriptures, he read about anointing with oil. He got a whole bottle of oil and poured the lot over his head, in the name of Jesus, and he was healed! Sometimes we get a little drop on our forehead; that's just a religious ceremony. This man believed that as he poured the lot over himself, he would be healed, and he was. I am sure that it was Three-In-One oil – Father, Son and Holy Spirit – good scriptural oil!

9. Praying More Than Once

This one is important for those people who have been prayed for before, and nothing's changed. First of all, if you have been prayed for, perhaps so many times that you have lost count, can I tell you that I appreciate your diligence in continuing to seek God. Let me encourage you and say you are very special. God's Word says very clearly that He is a rewarder of those who diligently seek Him (Hebrews 11:6). The person who goes on faithfully seeking God is somebody that God loves very much and He will reward. Every time I pray for a person, I believe that this is God's moment, no matter how many times they have been prayed for in the past.

> *'Then He came to Bethsaida; and they brought a blind man to Him, and begged Him to touch him. So He took the blind man by the hand and led him out of the town. And when He had spit on his eyes and put His hands on him, He asked him if he saw anything. And he looked up and said, "I see men like trees, walking." Then He put His hands on his eyes again and made him look up. And he was restored and saw everyone clearly.'*

(Mark 8:22–25).

This blind man was partially healed the first time Jesus prayed. He told Jesus he could see men like trees, walking. Lots of people I meet have been ministered to for healing and have been partly healed. Each one I have met had a choice on how they viewed the healing they received. Partial healing can be seen in one of two ways. You can say 'Why didn't He do the lot at once?' and begin to grumble. Like the children of Israel, murmuring and complaining is a sin many Christians are guilty of. The alternative is to get excited about healing you have received, however small it was.

Don't forget that there is a promise in the Word of God that says *'He who has begun a good work in you will complete it until the day of Jesus Christ.'* (Philippians 1:6). He is not going to stop, as we continue to seek Him.

What did Jesus do for the blind man? He prayed for him a second time and the man saw men as men. Jesus completed the work. If you have been prayed for once, you can be prayed for twice. To me twice could mean twenty-two, thirty-two, forty-two times; don't give up, don't lose heart.

God heals people; that's the basis on which we come to Him. Don't let anything put you off until you know you are healed.

10. Acting on Your Faith

*'Then as He entered a certain village, there met Him ten men who were lepers, who stood afar off. And they lifted up their voices and said, "Jesus, Master, have mercy on us!" So when He saw them, He said to them, "Go, show yourselves to the priests." And so it was that as they went, they were cleansed. Now one of them, when he saw that he was healed, returned, and with a loud voice glorified God, and fell down on his face at His feet, giving Him thanks. And he was a Samaritan. So Jesus answered and said, "Were there not ten cleansed? But where **are** the nine?"'*

(Luke 17:12–17).

We need to turn our eyes completely on Jesus and release our faith in Him, and believe Him to bring healing into our bodies. But what then? When you have been prayed for, obviously you have got to use your faith, because faith without works is dead. (James 2:20). Do you believe that? If you do, start to do the things you could not do before.

Let me illustrate. I often pray for people who have bad stomachs, ulcers and complaints that need special diets to keep them in control. Once I've prayed for these people I suggest that they find the nearest fish & chip shop, buy a portion of fish and chips, eat it and see that God has healed

24

them. It takes faith to do that, it's a risk, but you have to have corresponding action with your faith.

If your problem is arthritic knees, then after praying, use your faith and go for a jog. I've have seen folk start running and they've outrun me! If you have a bad back and it means you cannot bend down and touch your toes, do that as an act of faith.

The point I am making is that you need to use your faith. It doesn't just happen, you've got to do something – faith is a verb, a word describing action. Whatever the method of prayer for healing, faith has to come into operation. In many of the accounts of Jesus healing people, He says, 'Your faith has made you well.' The person doing the praying has got to have faith, but you have got to have faith too.

'Who Himself bore our sins in His own body on the tree, that we, having died to sins, might live for righteousness; by whose stripes you were healed.' (1 Peter 2:24).

The Cross of Jesus Christ is where God's blessing for us starts. You cannot get blessed unless you come to the Cross. It's because of the Cross of Jesus that you can be healed of your sickness. As Peter says it is by the stripes of Jesus that you are healed. The stripes refer to the wounds in Jesus' body; they were made by a cruel whip, when Jesus was flogged. All our suffering – our sickness, pain, disease, and oppression – was laid on Jesus. He is the source of our healing.

Coming to Jesus at the Cross is also the way we get healed spiritually. As I wrote in Chapter One, you can get into heaven in spite of a sick body, but you will never get into heaven with a sin sick soul. Jesus is the Healer, but He is also the Saviour. Before we go any further I want to ask you, 'Do you have an up-to-date, personal, intimate relationship with the Lord Jesus Christ as your Saviour and Lord? Have you been to the Cross by faith and seen that Jesus was nailed to the Cross for you? The blood which flowed from His wounds was for your personal forgiveness, from the sin that you have committed. Have you repented from your sin?' That means

'Have you taken responsibility for your personal sin?' Jesus went to the cross for your sins, as He did for mine, and you have to take the responsibility that your sin was the reason Jesus died.

Come to the Cross, confess, repent and turn away from that sinful nature. Let the blood of Jesus cleanse you and receive Jesus into your life. He wants to take control of your life, as you become His child, and enter His family. It is something you have to do on your own; no-one but you can take the responsibility.

Jesus said, *'Assuredly, I say to you, unless you are converted and become as little children, you will by no means enter the kingdom of heaven.'* (Matthew 18:3). You cannot get into heaven without conversion. You may be confirmed, but unless you are converted, your confirmation is a waste of time. The same is true for water baptism, unless you are converted, baptism is pointless. You may go to church and take the communion but without being a real follower of Christ it is meaningless. Conversion is unavoidable, and it starts with an act of your will.

We are going to take that first step to conversion right now.

If you want to become a Christian, to start living under the lordship of Jesus Christ I invite you to pray the following prayer, sincerely, from your heart:

'Thank you Lord Jesus for what you did, at the Cross, for me. I confess that I have sinned, but I do believe that you are the Son of God. You died on the Cross and shed your blood for me. I know that you were buried, but rose again from the dead.

As I now confess my sins I believe that they are forgiven. I repent and turn from my sin. I open my life to you and ask you to come, Lord Jesus, take control of my life and become my Lord. You are now the authority in my life and I give my whole life over to you.

Thank you Lord for hearing my prayer and coming into my life, today.

In the name of the Lord Jesus.   Amen.'

If you have prayed that prayer, I would like to hear from you. My address is

Evangelist Don Double,
Good News Crusade,
FREEPOST,
St Austell,
Cornwall, UK
PL25 4BR.

If you write, I will send back a Bible study booklet which will help you to further understand the important step you have taken.

Chapter 3

Healthy Emotions

'Whatever city you enter, and they receive you, eat such things as are set before you. And heal the sick who are there, and say to them, 'The kingdom of God has come near to you.''' (Luke 10:8–9).

When the Lord Jesus Christ commissioned His disciples to go out and extend His ministry, He set out clearly what they were to do. In these verses Jesus gave them two main commands to follow. They were to heal the sick and declare the good news of the Kingdom of God.

In each city they visited, they were to heal the sick. I believe that this command is still operative and we, as Jesus' disciples, should be obedient to His command. In whatever city we live our job is to heal the sick. The Word of God is that the sick **will** be healed. At the same time we are to declare that the Kingdom of God is near; the two commands should go hand in hand. Healing people is one way to prove to them that the Lord Jesus Christ, is the King. He is the One who is ruling and reigning and it is His Kingdom that comes near to us.

From the time that the disciples went out, the presence of the Kingdom of God has been announced to the world. Throughout the Gospels and the Book of Acts and on through the entire history of the Church, God's kingdom has been proclaimed as sick people have been healed in Jesus' name.

It's been almost two thousand years since Jesus spoke those

words. In that time we've seen a great advance in medical science; discoveries have been made that have brought healing to many people. But, we have to face the truth, **man's need is still as great as it has ever been**. There are probably more sick people in the world today than ever before; certainly as many people with heartaches, hurts and problems as there were in Jesus' day. We still need to **'go'** as Jesus commanded.

I want you to notice that Jesus said, 'Go and heal the sick.' He did not say, 'Go and heal the sicknesses.' There is a big difference; healing the sick and healing the sickness are not the same thing. You see, God is interested in you, as a whole person; He wants to remove the symptoms of sickness but He wants to do more than that, if you will allow Him. God is interested in you, this is a life changing fact that you need to get into your heart and mind. He knows your name, circumstances, pain, heartaches, and desires; everything there is to know about you.

Fruits and Roots

Most of the sick people I meet spend much of their time coping with the symptoms of sickness in their lives. The physical signs are usually evidence that there is something wrong inside. Sadly, too many people try to deal only with their symptoms but that is like lopping branches off a tree. I worked on a fruit farm, many years ago, and during the winter I pruned trees, just lopping off little branches. Our purpose was to make more wood which would eventually produce more fruit.

Pruning a tree did not kill it, but caused it to produce more fruit. To kill the tree you had to attack its roots. We need to do the same with sickness.

I believe that dealing with only the symptoms, is the reason why many people receive only temporary relief after prayer. Things get easier for a short time but then the pain returns. The source of 'life' for the symptoms is still growing. We need a radical solution that gets to the root and then the symptoms will 'dry up and wither.' God can go to the source of the problem and deal with it.

30

We are made in God's image, who is a triune being – Father, Son and Holy Spirit. In the same way man is made of three parts – body, soul, and spirit (1 Thessalonians 5:23). Sickness or disease in one part will affect the rest of our being. As the Healer, Jesus wants every part of us, body, soul and spirit to be in health. The Bible tells us that we are complete in Jesus. (Colossians 2:10). That is an accomplished fact, through the death of Jesus. However we need to realise that there is often a gap between our experience and the truth of God's word. We need to change our experience and bring our lives into line with God's word. All divine healing should bring us closer to living in the joy of completeness. In this chapter I want us to look at one area where most people need healing – our emotional lives.

The Lie of the Stiff Upper Lip

I have found that many physical symptoms are rooted in emotional problems and that when the emotions are straightened out the rest of our body comes into order. Our emotions are in our souls and given to us by God for a purpose. Sadly, many people seem to have a problem showing their emotions and expressing what they feel.

During an interview on Radio Norfolk, a journalist said to me, 'I have been along to one of your meetings and my problem is that there was a lot of emotion in what you did.' Emotionalism and misusing people's emotions is an accusation made at a lot of evangelists and all I can say is I want more emotion in my meetings if it brings people into a right relationship with God. It is impossible to be a Christian unless your emotions are involved.

You cannot be a Christian and not be emotional. Let me prove this from the scriptures. The Bible says unless you repent you will perish. That means that unless you repent you will go to hell. The Bible says *'Godly sorrow produces repentance.'* (2 Corinthians 7:10). In other words there has to be sorrow in our hearts, and in our lives, for us to repent and get right with God. Sorrow is an emotion; therefore the act of repenting has to involve your emotions.

31

The Bible is full of men and women who expressed real feeling in what they said and did. Not least among them was the Lord Jesus who very openly expressed His feelings of sorrow, joy, anger, and concern. That is very different from the behaviour of most English people. When confronted with crises we have been trained to present the 'stiff upper lip.' The British people admire those who can stay under pressure and not let on what they are really feeling; this is an unreal situation and can certainly produce sickness. Stifling our emotions can wound and hurt both ourselves and others, but praise God that He can set us free from such attitudes.

Jesus was a real man, and yet He openly wept at the death of his friend. (John 11:35). People say it is a sign of weakness to cry but that is a lie from Satan; I believe that it is a sign of strength and godliness. God wants to make you strong, therefore, He wants you to express your emotions.

Another great emotion is joy. We should be overflowing with joy, because the Bible says, 'The joy of the LORD is your strength' (Nehemiah 8:10); 'Therefore with joy you will draw water from the wells of salvation' (Isaiah 12:3), and 'In Your presence is fullness of joy; At Your right hand are pleasures forevermore.' (Psalms 16:11). If you are in the presence of God, there is joy.

We are to be people who rejoice. On one occasion the Bible says that the Lord Jesus, rejoiced in the Holy Spirit. (Luke 10:21). The Greek word that is translated 'rejoiced' literally means 'he leapt in the air!' Jesus was an emotional man and was not afraid to show it. I don't know where the idea came from that to be a Christian you have to be 'straight-laced,' but it certainly does not come from the Bible. To be a follower of Jesus involves using emotion and those emotions are good.

I want to make it clear that releasing and being free in our emotions is different from emotionalism, which is creating an emotional response just to have a nice feeling. God has given us emotions to use in order to express ourselves to Him and to one another, so be free.

When I pray for emotional healing in people, I often find that the Holy Spirit leads me to the same area of their thinking; it's the part of their emotions that handles how they relate and react with other people. It still amazes me how many sicknesses are caused because of relationship problems. For most people with emotional difficulties, it seems that if they could move to a desert island, most of their problems would immediately cease. There would be several new ones, but they would not have to relate to other people and so would not feel rejected. I am not suggesting that a desert island is the answer, because when He made Adam, God said, *'It is not good that man should be alone.'* (Genesis 2:18). We need healthy emotions so that we can relate together.

We live in a culture where 'the family' is falling apart; morality in our nation is decaying because of it. God wants to bring healing into relationships between husband and wife; between parents and children, (see Luke 1:17). In many churches the leaders and the congregation are separated by a rift that needs healing; and then there are hurts between fellow members of the Body of Christ. God wants us to be whole in our souls; I am convinced that a lot of physical sicknesses will disappear as a result.

Let's look at some of these emotional hurts and wounds which are so common in our generation:

Resentment

On one occasion a lady who had been divorced only days earlier came to me for help. She was almost hysterical and it was difficult to counsel her, but the Holy Spirit whispered in my ear the root of her problem. I said to her, 'Your problem is rejection,' and she immediately responded, 'Yes, I was rejected when I was six weeks old. My mother didn't want me and gave me away. I have never seen my mother since.' She went on to tell me of a life full of rejections, ending in her husband rejecting her in divorce. Her pain filled life had produced sickness. I had the joy of praying with her and asking the Lord Jesus to heal the hurts and wounds of all that rejection. As the Lord set her free, her face changed; it was like putting a light on in a dark room. She had held on to a lifetime of rejection and resented each one who had rejected her. By recognising what had happened and repenting, the Lord was able to heal and set her free. It was a beautiful sight.

People regularly say to me, 'Mr Double, it's true that I have been rejected but it is the other person who is at fault. They are the ones who need dealing with because they rejected me.' Now it maybe true that the other person was at fault and they are answerable to God for their actions. God will deal with them, *'Vengeance is Mine; I will repay, says the Lord.'* (Hebrews 10:30). However don't forget that you are the one who became rejected. Rejection always causes hurt and wounds and so you need healing. Holding on to a rejection breeds resentment; the fruit of resentment is always bitterness.

Bitterness

Science has proved that many types of arthritis, can be caused by bitterness and resentment. This is because your body reacts to what is happening in your emotions and dries up the fluid in your joints.

I saw this very vividly illustrated when a lady came to one of our crusade services. In my sermon I talked about being free from bitterness and resentment and at the end of the meeting she came forward for prayer. She knew she was bitter and resentful and wanted it dealt with. My colleague, Mike Darwood, prayed with her; she repented and asked God to forgive her bitterness. Mike asked God to take the root of bitterness out of her life. (When we pray with someone like this we always encourage the person to pray out loud and audibly speak forgiveness to the person they are forgiving. To be delivered from resentment means someone else has to be involved, the person who you need to forgive.) Arthritis had affected this lady from head to toe for twenty years, but she wasn't really concerned at that point about being healed. However, as she forgave, she immediately started to jump around, crying 'I'm healed, I am healed!' Every trace of arthritis had left her body the instant she forgave.

34

Grief and Disappointment

I have been told by doctors that some parts of the medical profession have established links between grief and diabetes. They tell me that as grief controls your emotions, it can affect your body by 'drying up' the cells that manufacture the insulin your body needs.

It has been my experience that at the root of much grief is disappointment. Now, I do not believe that it is God's will for anyone to ever be disappointed! That's worth repeating – I do not believe it is God's will for anyone to ever be disappointed. Now be careful, I did not say that you won't face disappointments. It is how you handle them that is important. When a disappointment comes, your first reaction, if you know the Lord, should be to know that *'he who believes in [Jesus] will not be disappointed.'* (Romans 9:33 New American Standard Bible; see also Romans 10:11 and Psalm 22:5) If you are disappointed, turn straight to Him and believe that scripture. With that attitude you will find that life is different. The other way of reacting to a disappointment is to welcome it, and begin to dwell on it. That way always produces hurt and a wound will open inside.

One of my favourite scriptures is Romans 8:28: *'And we know that all things work together for good to those who love God, to those who are the called according to His purpose.'* My understanding of that verse is that if you love God and know you are called according to His purpose, it is impossible for anything to go wrong. Again I am not being ridiculous, I am building my attitudes on the Word of God, so that when things appear to go wrong I know who is in control.

If I know that God is going to work good out of all of the events that come my way, I can look at a potential disappointment and relax that God is in control. I often greet friends and colleagues with 'It's the greatest day you ever lived.' That's not an empty catchphrase, it's the truth, if you are living in the reality of Romans 8:28.

Let me give you an illustration of living above our circumstances and seeing all things produce good for those God loves. A man who was a leader in an evangelical church, was

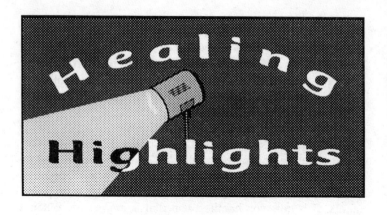

Teofila Conzaga

In January 1991 Don went to the Philippines to hold missionary crusades in two towns on the large southern island of Mindinao. The town of Dipilog was the site of the second crusade, and many people attended the crusade meetings and accepted Jesus as their saviour. There were a large number of notable healings during the crusade, including Teofila Conzaga.

She was brought to the stadium where the meetings were being held, on a stretcher. The local pastors described her as being 'out of her mind' as well as being paralysed. She laid on the stretcher listening to the service, and waiting for someone to pray for her.

As it was an evangelistic crusade Don preached the Gospel very clearly, proclaiming the lordship of Jesus Christ. As he did, demons started to leave Teofila. Nobody was directly praying for her, but as the Gospel was declared she was set free. Like the Gadarene man Jesus set free (Luke 8), she was 'demented' because of demonic activity. By the time Don had finished speaking she was in her right mind.

Then as people were being prayed for healing she got up from her stretcher and began to run around the front of the stadium. Don says, 'It was exciting to see the demons flee and then God touched her and made her whole.'

persuaded to come to one of our camps. Three miles from the camp site the engine of his car blew up and so he arrived at the camp on the back of a tow truck.

At our camps we divide into 'units' of seventy to one hundred people. Spending a week together as a unit encourages folk to share problems and prayer requests at a fairly deep level. This man, of course, had some big problems. He had a car with no engine, no money and no way to get his family home. He shared his problem with the unit leader who decided they would have some body ministry. The unit took a collection, believing that they would take enough money to buy a new engine. And they did!

Many of us think that body ministry is speaking in tongues, or prophesying or something else 'spiritual' but that is only a small part of the truth. Body ministry includes being able to share one another's needs. We belong to each other and can share one another's problems; we can suffer and rejoice with one another. Could you enjoy sharing another person's debts? I often do, it's a great joy to share someone's debts, and to help bless them. That is body ministry. (Now, before you start writing for help with your credit card bill please be aware of one point. I believe that if I can share in someone's debt it is also important that I tell them how not to get into debt again.)

Through the Body working, this man met with God in a new way and was baptised in the Holy Spirit. He went back to his church, which was quite small at the time, and started to share what he had learnt. The result was that the church was set on fire and revival came.

When his engine blew up, the man could have said 'It's all gone wrong,' and started to become depressed and disappointed. But the truth was that things were not going wrong, because God was working the circumstances for good. God was at work, He blessed a church with revival, through an engine blowing up! So do not let disappointment grip your life.

The Lord Jesus had an anointing and I believe His servants have that same anointing for the same ministry today. Two specific areas of Jesus' ministry were to heal the broken hearted and to set at liberty people who were oppressed.

(Luke 4:18). God wants to heal every broken heart and to set free the oppressed. The Greek word used in Luke 4 means, 'to be crushed by cruel oppression.' Jesus wants to set us free from the hurts and wounds that come from being crushed by cruel oppression.

If as you have been reading this, I've put my finger of something that is a 'sore spot,' realise that you can be free. To be free I believe you can pray, now, and as we learnt in chapter 1, reach out and touch the Lord. You may prefer to pray together with somebody, but however you pray, I suggest that you do it quickly.

As you have been reading, God may have put His finger on some area of your life where you need to forgive someone. That shows that God really does care about you and wants you to be completely whole. If you need to forgive someone there are four things to remember:

1: Forgiveness is an act of your will. Only you can make the decision to forgive.

2: Receive the ability to forgive. You need God's love, so open your heart and mind, and say 'Lord, fill me with your love.'

3: Speak out the forgiveness, audibly. Be specific, 'Mum, I forgive you.' 'John, I forgive you.'

4: Forgive, then forget. Forgetting means you won't dwell on that thought or allow it any room in your life.

Now let's pray. Please put the person's name, you are forgiving, in the blanks.

'Heavenly Father, thank you for the love you have for me. Thank you that it is consistent and never fails and that you are always wanting the very best for me.

Thank you for showing me this area of my life where I have been unforgiving. Lord, please give me the ability to forgive (name) _____

I receive your love to do that, right now.'

Now speak out that forgiveness:

(Name) _____

I forgive you for _____

Chapter 4

It's All In the Mind

I have been an Evangelist for over thirty years; in that time I have been to most parts of the British Isles and have prayed with thousands of people for their healing. Increasingly, I meet people whose sickness is not treatable by 'normal' science. Their symptoms are not caused by physical faults but rather they suffer from illnesses whose roots are in their mind.

The way that we think and the attitudes we have do affect our health. This was confirmed by my doctor, when he told me, 'Don, you can do more to help fifty percent of the people who come into my surgery than I can ever do. The problem is that many people have nothing to believe in and lack self-assurance.' He is right. The truth is that we all need something to believe in, and if there is nothing we can direct our belief at, our imagination will create something. This is at the heart of most psychosomatic illness.

Many things affect the way we think and the attitudes we hold, some good and some bad. The negative events like rejection and abuse can result in a mental wound that shows itself in physical symptoms. This type of sickness often means that the doctors can do very little medically; Valium and similar tranquilizers only deaden the mental anguish but do little to bring real healing.

Psychosomatic sicknesses are very real; they can take root very easily through things like rejection. The seeds of rejection come in many forms; perhaps your parents rejected you, or your spouse walked out, or your school teachers told you that you would never be any good. These negative actions and words are like seeds sown into our lives.

People in this position usually try to compensate for their rejection by getting someone to pay attention to them. It may be a subconcious action but what they are saying is, 'Hey, look I am here, I want you to recognise me.' Without other people sympathising with them, many hypochondriacs feel that they would go unnoticed.

This kind of rejection can happen through the smallest of incidents. For instance, how do you react when you are ignored by someone as you enter a room? It is possible that a 'minor' hurt like not saying 'Hello,' can produce crippling psychosomatic illnesses.

I have prayed with people who were convinced they had a cancer. They have had every symptom – pain and even swelling, but the doctors have given them all tests and there was no trace of cancer or anything similar. It was purely in their mind and the root was rejection and inner hurt. They just needed attention. If they could not get attention from those close to them, the attention and sympathy of a doctor or a nurse had to suffice.

I am told that varicose veins are often manifestations of hurt and rejection. An ulcerated vein demands a lot of careful attention, looking after dressings etc. Now, although not all varicose veins are the result of mental stress, it is very interesting that one of the groups who suffer most from this complaint are middle aged and older women. Often their families are growing up, children are establishing their own personalities, and the mother finds her purpose in life has gone. When the children were younger she was the centre of their world, now she's not, but she still wants and needs attention.

If you recognise yourself in something I have shared so far, know that you can be completely set free from your hurts and rejections. The Bible says that Jesus was *despised and rejected by men, a man of sorrows and acquainted with grief.'* (Isaiah 53:3). He was rejected for us. Jesus became a substitute for everything that we are, so that we can become everything that He is.

I would suggest that all psychosomatic sicknesses have their main roots in fear. Again, doctors tell us that one of the main causes of blood pressure is repressed fear; fear that is pushed down, suppressed and ignored. Remember that we are body, soul and spirit, not three separate parts but a unity. Sadly when you hide fear and push it down in your emotional life, you can push up your blood pressure.

There was a time when I was very fearful, I was almost afraid of being afraid! It was a ghastly state to be in but, praise God, over the years I have been delivered from many fears. God seems to have chosen, in His own sovereign will, that the fears should surface at different times so that I could be delivered. Let me encourage you with my own testimony.

When I started in ministry I had a massive inferiority complex. It was rooted in my lack of education, through having TB as a boy and missing school. While ministering at a conference, in one session the speaker had a word of knowledge to which I responded. He told me that I had an inferiority complex spirit, which was rooted in fear. I had never heard of such a spirit, in fact I regarded my inferiority as something of a virtue; I thought I was being humble. However, I agreed that the man could pray for me and I was instantly and wonderfully delivered. In the past when another preacher was around I tried to hide and take a back seat. On that day God showed me that the Holy Spirit in me is as good as the Holy Spirit in anyone else. It is Him and His anointing that counts, and since then I have never worried about who is around, God set me free.

Another fear that I needed release from was sown in me by a letter which contained a negative 'prophecy' regarding my past life. This prophecy took root and I began to fear that God was going to 'get' me and judge me. The way this fear showed itself, was that whenever I went overseas to minister I would get sick. I recognised that this only affected me when I was overseas, so with my colleague Mike Darwood we agreed to pray and ask God to deliver me from this thing before our next trip. One day just before leaving, I was in the bath and God spoke to me, showing me the roots of the problem were in this 'prophecy.' After dressing, I immediately rang Mike and he came and prayed for me. The fear was dealt with and since then, whenever I have travelled abroad, I have not been affected by the same kind of illness.

From the day I was born I have had a dreadful fear of water, so much so that I wouldn't even go under a shower unless I had to and I certainly couldn't swim. I would always try to get someone else to wash my hair so that I could hold a towel over my face, as I could not bear water around my face. One day Mike Darwood was praying with me about something totally unrelated and God gave him a word of knowledge regarding this fear. Something had happened as I was being born that had registered in my mind and had given a place for fear to take root. Mike prayed, casting out the fear and I have enjoyed the pleasures of showering and washing my own hair from that day on. I have started to learn to swim, and gone down a seventy foot water chute into a pool; not bad for a man in his fifties!

One verse that has greatly encouraged me is in Psalm 34. It says:

> *'I sought the LORD, and He heard me,*
> *And delivered me from all my fears.'*   (Psalm 34:4)

Some Christians would say God allows us certain fears, which we should use as a challenge, but I believe God wants us free from every irrational fear. There is a wonderful scripture we need in this context:

> *'For God has not given us a spirit of fear, but of power and*
> *of love and of a sound mind.'*   (2 Timothy 1:7)

If God did not give you your fears, where did they come from? From Satan! God did not give us a spirit of fear, but He does give us something, in fact three things – *Love*, *Power* and a *Sound Mind*. Let's look at these in a bit more detail:

Love

'There is no fear in love; but perfect love casts out fear, because fear involves torment. But he who fears has not been made perfect in love.'   (1 John 4:18).

Fill yourself with love and fear will flee from your life. It is true, like oil and water, fear and love can't be mixed; so by filling yourself with love, fear has to go. That is why I don't like horror films, which sow seeds of fear. It is far better to focus on love.

Love is not just a passive thing, love has to have a way to express itself. I know people whose lack of health is caused by not loving in a positive way. You may be like them; if so, know that you can change.

Love needs to express itself. Take your Bible and read 1 Corinthians, chapter 13; the definition of love you find there is full of activity. You need to go out and love people. Find people to love and give yourself to them, because love serves people and in loving others you cannot be self-centred. Don't always look to people to do things for you, but go out and love them. If somebody rejects your love, don't stop, find somebody else to love.

David du Plessis speaking on the fruit of the spirit listed in Galatians chapter 5 said a very profound thing. He said, 'Fruit grows on trees, and once you've grown a fruit, you harvest it.' The fruit of the Spirit should be like that in our lives. Let me illustrate: John has grown a fruit of the Spirit, Love. He has a ripe Love fruit growing on his tree. I come along and really irritate him, by doing something that annoys him. Now, he has a choice. Does he let me see how annoyed he is, or does he use the fruit he's grown? On this occasion he doesn't allow his irritation to ruffle him, but reaches out and uses the fruit of love. He says, 'Don, I would like to take you out for lunch and buy you a nice meal. Where do you want to go?' After enjoying a five course meal and having a wonderful time it's clear that the fruit of the Spirit does work. John has loved me and I've benefited from the fruit. What you also need to see is that I have that seed of love in my life. If I choose, it can grow

Pat Smith

For more than twenty years Pat suffered with arthritis. It started in her neck and spine and so the doctors put her through various treatments, including traction, to alleviate the pain – all without success.

The disease slowly spread, finally affecting her hands. They became so weak that she kept dropping things and had to wear wrist supports. Her life became a struggle against constant pain. During the day it hurt to move and at night she couldn't sleep properly because she couldn't get comfortable.

Then one of her children saw an advert in their local paper announcing that a local fellowship were having a 'Miracle Crusade.' Although none of the family were Christians they encouraged her to go along. With nothing to lose she decided to try it and went along to the service.

Don Double was the visiting speaker, and after he had preached she asked for prayer. He laid hands on her and prayed in the Name of Jesus for healing. She says 'I felt something deep, deep down inside myself and now I am entirely free of pain. I find it hard to believe. The warden in the sheltered home where I live came and said "What have you done Pat? You look so different!" I had to tell her what had happened and said "I am not in pain. I've got my bounce back again. I feel so different!"'

Since then Pat has become a Christian, and is still enjoying God's healing.

another crop in me; that is how we need to keep filled with love. Love is there for us to use. Use love by serving, blessing, giving. To do that we have to keep on growing new crops of the fruit of love for others to come and pick; in that way we will benefit from it ourselves.

Power

God has given us love but He has also given us power. That gives us authority, so when Satan tries to attack us, we can say 'Get behind me Satan; fear, you have no place in me.'

When we have power, we also have ability to go where fear has dominated. Fears and phobias, like agoraphobia, have to go as we declare the power of Jesus. As that spirit is broken, the next thing to do is to replace it with the Holy Spirit's love and power.

When I pray for people about phobias, I encourage them to start doing the things they couldn't; in the case of agoraphobia it would be to go out into open spaces. The day after praying for a lady to be delivered from agoraphobia, I was out doing a bit of shopping. Suddenly from the other side of the road someone shouted, 'Mr. Double. Look, I am out, all on my own!' It was the lady I had prayed for. What was she doing? She was positively using the power God had given her.

It is no good being prayed for and then saying, 'I wonder what's happened, let's see if I am healed.' With that attitude you will never be healed. After prayer, move out in what God has given you. It's called using your faith!

A Sound Mind

The third thing God has given us is a sound mind, something we all need. It is a fact that we can live with less than a sound mind, although God has given us one; that's one of the affects of sin. But, praise God, Jesus made a way at Calvary for us to regain a sound mind. Hypochondria and things like phobias, anxiety and worry are all related; they all indicate that our mind isn't working properly. You might have an educated mind, but that is no guarantee that you have a sound mind. In fact it is quite possible that the opposite is true – I am told that the highest suicide rate in the western world is among psychiatrists!

The only way to have a sound mind is to think the way God thinks. You need your mind programmed like God, to think the way He thinks and to speak the way He speaks.

'Do not be conformed to this world, but be transformed by the renewing of your mind, that you may prove what is that good and acceptable and perfect will of God.'

(Romans 12:2)

The way we get our mind renewed is by allowing the Word of God to dwell in us richly. (Colossians 3:16) Practically that means to read God's word, meditate on it, learn it, be filled with it and begin to think God's Word; all of which will produce a sound mind.

Jesus commanded us not to worry. (Matthew 6:25, 31, & 34) Worrying is perhaps the most common evidence of fear. In my travels around the world I have come to the conclusion that worry is an English trait, we worry about all kinds of things. But we are not to be conformed to this world, we should have our minds transformed by the Holy Spirit.

What is worry? One definition which I think is very accurate is that it is 'unholy meditation.' Worrying is often not intelligent, because it is like fertilizer for our fears. As we worry those fears grow. Jesus in telling the parable of the Sower described the 'cares of the world,' the things we worry about, as thorns. (Mark 4:19). Instead of this unholy meditation we should spend time thinking like Paul told the Philippians:

'Finally, brethren, whatever things are true, whatever things are noble, whatever things are just, whatever things are pure, whatever things are lovely, whatever things are of good report, if there is any virtue and if there is anything praiseworthy; meditate on these things.'

(Philippians 4:8)

We need to have our whole lives filled up with peace and harmony. A sound mind will not allow room for anything else. Obeying Philippians 4:8 will go a long way to bringing peace and harmony into our lives. What do I mean when I use the word harmony? The opposite of harmony is discord. In our lives discord happens when we are out of relationship with God or other people. If I am not right with my wife I am in discord, and there is no harmony, no peace.

An incident from the life of a well known evangelist illustrates this point very well. One day he had a little tiff with his wife just before he went to preach at the mid-week service. He was late, and so without resolving the issue with his wife, he put on his coat, picked up his Bible, said goodbye and left. As he was walking down the path, God spoke to him, 'Where are you going son?' He replied, 'You know where I am going Lord, I am going to speak at the mid-week service.' So God said 'Are you? You may be going to the service, but I am staying in the kitchen with your wife!' He had to go back and sort things out with his wife, then the peace and harmony came back.

'Do not touch My anointed ones, and do My prophets no harm.' (1 Chronicles 16:22). A major disruption to peace and harmony is criticism. This is particularly so when we speak against our church leaders. Most men who minister in any form of public ministry will say something, at some time, that irritates a group of listeners. The rest of his ministry may be extraordinary, and yet just one or two points of disagreement bring his whole ministry into question. This is 'touching' God's anointed. When that happens it is not God's man that is harmed, it's the criticiser who is hurt often with sickness. You are allowed to disagree with someone but don't attack them personally or criticise or speak evil of them. I am amazed how often the Lord has blessed me for determining to stay in harmony even when I have strongly disagreed with other brothers; the principle does work.

All sickness brings a degree of turmoil into our lives. In fact the word we use, 'dis-ease' conveys the idea that all is not right with our bodies. Jesus said 'My peace I give to you.' (John 14:27). The peace Jesus gives is genuine and heals you.

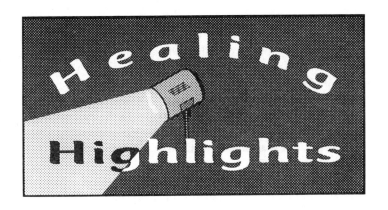

Peter Long

Peter was a keen runner. Imagine his frustration when he broke his foot in an accident. Unfortunately it was made worse because as the bones in his foot healed, they 'solidified' together. This obviously curtailed his running.

At a Good News Crusade mission in Norfolk, near to where Peter lived Don prayed for him. He said it felt as if boiling water was being poured over him (in a pleasant sort of way!) As Don mentions elsewhere in this book, it was time for faith and action to work together. The mission tent was sited in a large field and so Don told Peter to go for a run around the field, which he promptly did, completing four circuits before stopping! Isn't God good?

One final point on harmony. When a choir sings in close harmony, they don't sing the same notes, they all sing different parts which together blend into a beautiful harmony. Harmony in our lives comes as we see our place in life and make our contribution to the whole. We will be at harmony when our body, soul and spirit are working together.

I have a big family – not only five children, but we have had an extended family as well. Sometimes there have been up to ten or twelve people living in the house and most of the time we have had beautiful peace and harmony. But there have been times when pressures have built up and people became irritated or annoyed. It is hard to live in such an atmosphere; it brings so many problems of disharmony. In the end we learnt to deal with things straight away, not sweeping disputes 'under the carpet.' Peace reigned again when everyone played their part properly.

God has no failures. There are no failures in the Body of Christ. God made every person for a purpose and as we find the place that God has for us we will discover that our contribution has been used as part of a beautiful harmony. However even more than that, there is harmony inside when I am doing what God wants me to do. The will of God is comfortable; to me that type of harmony brings health.

Chapter 5

Don's Guide to Healthy Living

Although healing is important, I am sure that God's best for us is not healing! Instead He wants us to live in **health**. Note what the following scripture says:

> '*My son, give attention to my words; incline your ear to my sayings. Do not let them depart from your eyes; keep them in the midst of your heart; For they are life to those who find them, and health to all their flesh.*'
>
> (Proverbs 4:20–22)

The Bible is clear; God's words need to be kept before our eyes and in our hearts, constantly. They will be health and healing to us; therefore our relationship with God, and His Word, is the most important in our life.

I do not wish to be unkind but the truth is that people often miss God by 'running' after ministries and people with gifts. I've seen too many people who are repeatedly disappointed and frustrated still looking for the 'cure.' Sadly, they've missed the foundation of their healing and health – God's Word. The more we allow God's Word to dwell in us, the more health we will have and that is always better than healing.

3 John 2 makes it clear that it is God's will for us to be in health and to prosper, even as our soul prospers. That is God's plan for us. We can live consistently in health. To live like that we need to give attention to the temple of the Holy Spirit, our body.

'Do you not know that you are the temple of God and that the Spirit of God dwells in you? If anyone defiles the temple of God, God will destroy him. For the temple of God is holy, which temple you are.'

(1 Corinthians 3:16–17)

God lives in individuals and in the Church. We are His temple both individually and collectively. In applying this scripture to us as individuals it is clear that if we defile the temple, our bodies, God will destroy us. In many ways destruction is certainly a sickness; when my body is sick, it can feel as if it is falling apart.

In the Old Testament, the Temple was given the very highest priority and care. The people of Israel gave their best to build and decorate it, and it was really looked after. We neglect our temple of God when we mistreat it or we underestimate its value. I want to use my body, my temple, to express the life of God to others. For it to be usable I need to keep myself in good condition, at my best for God.

Look at the shelves of any High Street bookshop and you will quickly discover a obsession with health. Hundreds of books have been published, full of diets and exercise plans all promising to help us get fit and healthy. Health is big business, today. Yet if you read your Bible, you will find that God got there first! Health was His idea and He gives us plenty of pointers on living the right way. The problem is most people don't know what God's word says about a healthy lifestyle, and ignore His guidance.

'Hear, my son, and be wise; and guide your heart in the way. Do not mix with winebibbers, or with gluttonous eaters of meat; for the drunkard and the glutton will come to poverty, and drowsiness will clothe a man with rags.'

(Proverbs 23:19–21)

The Bible speaks about God's people needing wisdom. The Apostle James wrote, *'If any of you lacks wisdom, let him ask of God, who gives to all liberally and without reproach, and it will be given to him.'* (James 1:5). We all need wisdom to know the best lifestyle and out of that wisdom will come health.

Lack of wisdom is easily noticed. Proverbs 23:19–21 mentions two ways it is manifest and directs us not to mix with drunkards or gluttons. Most Christians have an opinion about the use and abuse of alcohol. For some it is sin to drink any alcohol at all; a rule that is imposed with strict legalism. Yet, few people have the same attitude to eating as they do to drinking. The Bible, however, does link the two and regards greed in eating as an equal sin to drunkenness. (Look at Romans 13:13; 1 Peter 4:3; Proverbs 30:21–22.) We need to have the same balance that the Word of God has about drinking and eating. Whilst normal eating and drinking is not sinful, over eating or gluttony, and drunkenness is. The practical affects of this type of lifestyle is something I can speak of with experience.

Some time ago I fell over and sprained my ankle. The pain and discomfort continued for some months and in that time all sorts of people prayed for me. After a while I got used to the pain and I refused to feel 'down' about it; ten months later it still wasn't properly healed and my ankle was very swollen. Then God spoke to me and said very clearly, 'Your problem is that you are overweight.'

For several years I had tried to get my weight down. My wife and friends had spoken to me about it, even my doctor had suggested a diet and so I struggled and lost a few pounds. But they soon went back on again. When God spoke it was different. One of the things I make sure I always do when God speaks to me is to obey. You don't get an option when God speaks. So, it was time to lose weight but I had tried several diets and all had had the same affect. For a while I lost weight but then it went back on again and I was back to square one.

I decided that there were two things that needed to happen. If God had told me to lose weight, He wouldn't leave me to struggle by myself. He would help me, and that is what happened. This led to the second step which came in a word of wisdom. I needed to make a radical change in my eating habits. Not so much what I ate, but when I ate. Many of us who spend a lot of time travelling, preaching the Gospel, get forced into an unhealthy routine. Most preachers don't like ministering on full stomachs, and so we eat our biggest meal of the day at 11 o'clock at night. I often ate a three course meal at that time and then went to bed, full. Doctors will tell you eating like that is a guaranteed way to put on weight.

With so much excess weight I got to the point where I wanted to be asleep more than I was awake. I would get out of breath whilst preaching. So I made a decision to change my eating habits, eating the main meal of the day at lunchtime. Combined with a balanced diet I lost 50lbs in four months. It was like being born again! I felt a new man and, praise God, I am still enjoying the benefits of being lighter. If eating is a problem for you, do not despair. The Lord is interested in you; He will give you the wisdom to know how to lose weight and also how to keep it off.

For me, my relationship with Jesus is very practical, even to the point of helping me diet. God designed me, He knows how I can function and, like an expert mechanic, He can guide me in keeping my body in peak condition. Find out what a good weight for you is; make sure you are around that weight. With God you can do it.

One of the reasons people over-eat is because they are lonely. I know some folk who are permanently depressed because they are lonely. Once I prayed for a man who was addicted to 'Mars Bars.' He ate them continuously, not because he was hungry, but because he was depressed. By tackling the root of the problem, the rejection that caused him to be lonely, we provided a way out of the symptom of depression.

Over-eating, especially eating between meals, is a clear sign of a lack of discipline in a person's life. Healthy people are disciplined people. It is not a mistake that part of the fruit of the Holy Spirit is self-discipline. We need to face these facts and to see that gluttony is a sin.

The second practical area of healthy living is Exercise. People are sick because of the lack of exercise. In Paul's first letter to Timothy he says, *'For bodily exercise profits a little, but godliness is profitable for all things, having promise of the life that now is and of that which is to come.'* (1 Timothy 4:8). Unfortunately, some people read that verse and dismiss all forms of exercise saying it only profits a little. Surely we need all the good we can get?

In the Twentieth century with the invention of the motor car and a wide range of 'labour saving' devices it's easy to become lazy. We need to keep our body in order by exercising it. Even a simple thing like walking instead of taking the car, is a good step (excuse the pun!). Every morning before I dress, I always spend about ten minutes doing some exercise, which I have found helps me be alert mentally as well as physically waking me up. Many people are sluggish when reading the Word because their minds are not alert. Exercise can help you be alert and I would strongly recommend it as a practical contribution to your health.

The next area of healthy living is the opposite of exercise – Rest.

Before I talk about resting let me say that too many people quote the fifth commandment wrongly. It says:

> *'Remember the Sabbath day, to keep it holy. Six days you shall labour and do all your work, but the seventh day is the Sabbath of the LORD your God. In it you shall do no work: you, nor your son, nor your daughter, nor your male servant, nor your female servant, nor your cattle, nor your stranger who is within your gates. For in six days the LORD made the heavens and the earth, the sea, and all that is in them, and rested the seventh day. Therefore the LORD blessed the Sabbath day and hallowed it.'*
>
> (Exodus 20:8–11)

Too often I hear people quote these verses, putting the emphasis on the resting, ignoring the first part of the verse. It says you **shall** labour for six days to get one day of rest. A working week of six days will do no one any harm! When I was younger the working week was a lot longer than it is today; ten hours a day, five days a week and about five hours on Saturday

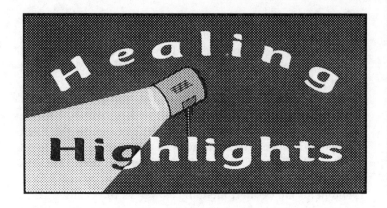

Marjorie Chamberlain

'When I was one year old I had Polio, which damaged my body and has affected me ever since. At the age of 13 I had to have surgery and later had to wear callipers to help me walk. I was like that for thirty eight years, until 1980 when I had another operation. The result of the op. was that I could walk without the callipers, but I did need to use a stick. The result of all this was that I contracted arthritis in my legs, which was very painful.

In May 1990 Don Double was holding a mission at Cheam Park, Surrey. On the 16th May I went along and asked for the team to pray for me for healing. God touched me and healed me of the arthritis in my legs.

Almost a year later I am still walking around without pain and without a stick – the arthritis has gone. The wasted muscles have still not come to life yet, but in my heart I am just praising the Lord for all His goodness to me and for His joy and peace in my heart.'

was normal. It is my opinion that physically people were healthier as a result.

Now, I am not arguing for a return to the 'good old days,' but I think we do need to be aware that all our modern inventions mean that far more people work sitting down. We need to make sure we compensate for this lack of physical activity. I know of one minister who recommends that men who have 'desk' jobs, find something they can do manually, for even a short period, every day. That is good advice.

The fifth commandment specifies that in any week six days are for work, labour, and the remaining day is a day of rest. So, to rest is obeying God's will. How do we do that?

Gordon McDonald in his excellent book *Ordering Your Private World* has some good things to say on this subject. I am indebted to him for some of the thinking he provoked in my life. When the Bible talks about rest, what do you think of? McDonald puts forward the idea that in the latter part of the Twentieth century the word 'rest' has become distorted from its original meaning. Rest has been largely substituted by what we call Leisure.

In this country there is a multi-million pound leisure industry. Leisure is now big business. All kinds of facilities have been built, inviting us to spend our 'leisure time' engaged in a wide range of activity. There is nothing wrong with leisure or fun and pleasure but we must not substitute it for rest. Today we have more time not working than our fathers and grandfathers and yet we seem more fatigued in our bodies and our minds.

Gordon McDonald suggests that leisure is only a 'temporary lifter.' Rest, however, has a permanent affect on us that should penetrate to the deepest level of a person's inner life. This type of fatigue is rarely, if ever, touched by any of the modern leisure activities.[1]

As I read this book I felt God spoke to me about my day off, or Sabbath. Now, my Sabbath is not Sunday, because as a

[1] The relevant chapter is Chapter 14 Rest beyond Leisure (p.173). *Ordering Your Private World*, Gordon McDonald, Highland Books 1985

preacher that is a day when I am always busy. But I still need a day of rest, a day of relaxation, a day when I can have a change and perhaps do nothing. Here is a big challenge, are you the kind of person who can sit and do nothing? Or must you always be doing something, even if it is knitting or something like that? Can you just sit and relax and just enjoy God, and His presence? That is what we need to be able to do; enjoying a rest that penetrates every area of fatigue in our lives.

A few years ago I was on holiday in Tunisia. My wife Heather had taken the family to get ice-creams, and I was lying by the swimming pool enjoying the heat of the sun. It was about 90 degrees in the shade and lovely. As I was lying there, God spoke to me. He said, 'Don, I am enjoying you doing nothing.' For about two hours I meditated on that and I began to see the wonder of God enjoying me doing nothing.

So many of us get the idea that we can only please God when we are rushing around. We must witness, pray, read the Bible, or do something to stay in God's 'good books.' Because we are so busy we don't hear God whisper, 'I enjoy you doing nothing.' Understanding that changed my life. Having just read *Ordering Your Private World*, this thought had an even greater impact, God can really enjoy me doing nothing. He created me and made me for Him.

Too often what we call godly activity, is really only satisfying us instead of satisfying God. We need to be able to rest; this is a challenge – put a little bit of rest into your life. I am convinced that if you do, you will have more health than you ever had before. By dealing with the fatigue in your life you will go a long way to leading a healthier life.

Relaxation is the key, and is one of the reasons things like T.M. and Yoga have caught on. God wants us to relax, but the sad fact is that Satan has substituted 'answers,' like Transcendental Meditation, that result in people being taken further from God. The atmosphere we create around ourselves is crucial to this, and it starts with our attitudes. If our attitudes are based on God's word we can cultivate an atmosphere of peace. Peace from any source other than Jesus, the Prince of Peace, is in the end not peace at all, but a false calm.

In our society 'stress' is a major killer. There are many diseases that have been linked to stress; these include heart attacks, high blood pressure, ulcers and mental breakdowns. Every year the list seems to get longer. Most doctors are of the opinion that if you are a person who is susceptible to stress, and you find it hard to relax, you have increased the chances of suffering one of these illnesses.

Do you live under stress and tension? Then read this next section carefully. The Bible says we are not to worry, be anxious, or have fear. You may reply 'It's easy to read the words, but impossible to do.' Read the words of Jesus:

> *'Therefore I say to you, do not worry about your life, what you will eat or what you will drink; nor about your body, what you will put on. Is not life more than food and the body more than clothing?'* (Matthew 6:25)

> *'Therefore do not worry about tomorrow, for tomorrow will worry about its own things. Sufficient for the day is its own trouble.'* (Matthew 6:34)

Note that Jesus' words are not optional, he is giving us a command. Therefore it is important to see that worrying has a lot to do with our will. By an act of my will I can decide to be obedient to God's word, and **not worry**.

I remember a preacher saying, 'If you worry, you die. If you don't worry, you die. So why worry?' That makes a lot of sense. Controlling anxiety and worry starts by getting your inner life under control. That act of your will is so important because only you can stop yourself from getting anxious. I am still working on this, and I'm improving all the time but it takes hard work.

Worry and anxiety are symptoms of our modern life. People do it almost without thinking! It's normal to worry, and yet Jesus told us not to. Jesus' main theme in Matthew chapter 6 is that you don't worry what you are going to wear, and you don't worry what you're going to eat. Don't worry about the simplest things in life. Jesus pointed to a field lily growing in the grass near to where he was sitting. It was probably

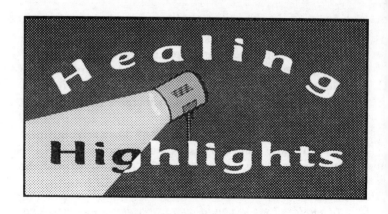

Peter Ward

'I was diagnosed as having a hernia early in 1987 and I was duly booked for an operation. However, in July of the same year, I went along to the Bow Mission held by the Good News Crusade. At the close of the meeting I went forward for prayer for healing. God touched me and healed me of my hernia.

On 5th January 1988 I was examined by my own doctor, who verified that there was no trace of the hernia and agreed that it had been healed by God. The forthcoming operation was cancelled.

This, by the way increased my faith in the healing power of God. It has greatly assisted me receiving the ministry of healing and deliverance that I believe I have been called into by the Lord Jesus, and I am still healed, praise the Lord!'

something like the daisies that grow in our lawns. He pointed to the flower and said, *'it does not toil, does not spin and yet Solomon in all his glory wasn't as beautiful as one of these.'* The daisy just grows because God made it to do that and it does a good job of it. God says that is how we should live; by our simple trust and faith in God, we should let God provide for us and not get worried.

This can be a challenge, because the implications are enormous. How many people struggle and strive, just to 'keep up with the Joneses?' There are pressures to buy this, and get that, and if you don't, you won't live a full life. Living the Jesus way means going against the tide, living a very different life from our neighbours. However there is a reward, because if we don't worry about all these things, we leave room for God to bless us with His abundance. I'm convinced that like the daisies, and the sparrows, if we give God the control of our lives, He will adequately provide for us.

I heard a man say one day, 'We take our life far too seriously,' and he's right. We take life far too seriously, because we think life is serious. I'm sure that was why Jesus upset so many of the Pharisees; they wanted Him to be more serious than He was. They thought that being holy meant observing the Law. When Jesus came along and suggested that all they were doing was empty religion and a waste of time the religious leaders were not happy!

Religion has done untold harm to Christians ever since. It has tried to push people into a way of thinking that is not what Jesus taught. Recently I met a pastor of a church who had organised a 'Make Way' celebration; his church had paraded down their High Street, throwing balloons and streamers, and singing joyful songs. He had got some people to produce placards which read:–

DOWN WITH RELIGION – UP WITH JESUS

I think we should all wear badges with that on. Religion makes us take life far too seriously. God made us to enjoy what He created and enjoy him. It is time we began to do that;

I know I am enjoying living now. As a friend of mine said, 'I don't want to go to heaven yet, I am enjoying it far too much here!' Satan's plan is that we get full of stress and anxiety and worry. Jesus came to give us life, and life in all its abundance. (John 10:10). He wants us free from stress and that starts when we stop taking life so seriously and being so intense. As Tony Campolo says, 'The kingdom of God is a party!'

Chapter 6

Total Healing –
The Will of God For You

For many people God's will is a thing that is very difficult to understand; the reasons why God does things in a certain way are a mystery to them. Nowhere is this more true than in the area of healing, and yet God has revealed in His Word what His will is.

Much of the confusion in people's minds comes from the instances where people ask God for healing, but don't seem to get healed. One name that immediately comes to mind is that of David Watson, perhaps the most gifted Evangelist the UK has seen since the War. David Watson contracted cancer and because he was well-known, tens of thousands of ordinary people prayed for his healing. He appeared on TV and radio, declaring that God was going to heal him, because He had promised to do so. When David died, many people's faith was severely challenged. I've met people who have said to me, 'If David Watson did not get healed, God won't heal me.'

There have been other well-known ministers who have died through illness, and their deaths have caused people to start falling apart. I knew David Watson, and I am sure that he, and many other godly men who have died prematurely, would want to stand by God's Word. In spite of what happened to them, we must base our understanding on God's word, and not on the experiences of other people.

The Word of God is the starting point for finding out what God's will is; there is no difference between God's will and

God's Word. When looking for God's will on the subject of healing my starting point is Psalm 103:3

> '... *Who forgives all your iniquities, Who heals all your diseases,* ...'

In Spurgeon's commentary on the Psalms, *The Treasury of David*, he makes a very profound statement. 'That little word "all" means "all." If God heals all your diseases it could not possibly mean "all, except the one I've got."' He also makes it clear that the Hebrew word which we translate 'diseases,' does include sickness in our bodies. This is the Word of God; whatever anyone else thinks or feels or experiences, He heals **all** of our diseases.

As Jesus travelled around Palestine, we read that He healed people by rebuking the devil. When he healed the sick He laid the responsibility for their sickness at Satan's door. I do not believe that God blesses people with sickness. In fact Jesus said his Father delighted in giving good things to His children:

> '*If you then, being evil, know how to give good gifts to your children, how much more will your Father who is in heaven give good things to those who ask Him!*'
>
> (Matthew 7:11)

I would certainly never 'bless' any of my children with cancer and if I am like that my Heavenly Father is much better. He certainly would not 'bless' His children with sickness or disease.

To be in God's will is the most important thing in my life. If it is God's will for me to be sick, then I want to be sick, but I don't believe that is God's will. God's will for me is to be healthy.

Let's just contrast this with the issue of Salvation. When we preach the Gospel does every sinner get saved? I wish that were true, but it isn't, yet the Bible makes it quite clear that '*The Lord is* ... *not willing that any should perish but that all should come to repentance.*' (2 Peter 3:9). It is His will that everybody should be saved, but not everyone is. The same is true for healing. We preach that everybody can be healed, but everyone who gets prayed for does not get healed, and yet that does not mean that God's will has changed.

At this point I want to make a comment about the medical profession. If it was God's will for people to be sick, the doctor, nurse and chemist would be out of God's will. But I believe that they are working in accord with the will of God, because they are trying to get people healed. Some of the techniques some doctors use may be questionable, however the principle is there; God wants us healthy, Satan is the author of disease.

I often meet people who tell me that it is not God's will to heal them, and yet they will happily go down to the doctor's surgery, to get a prescription for tablets or whatever. There is a problem of logic in this because the fact that a person goes to the doctor means that in their heart of hearts they don't really believe they should be ill. If they don't believe they should be sick, why don't they believe that it is God's will for them to be healed?

When I'm sick I will always ask for someone to pray for me. If I'm healed immediately, marvellous, but if I'm not I will go to the Doctor. That is not lack of faith, I go believing that God will heal me using the skills the doctor has.

'God anointed Jesus of Nazareth with the Holy Spirit and with power, who went about doing good and healing all who were oppressed by the devil, for God was with Him.' (Acts 10:38). Jesus was battling with the oppression of the devil when He was healing the sick. One of the things I have learnt about oppression is that it is full of lies. When people are oppressed, the Truth will set them free because it is lies from the Father of Lies, that try to push them down; that is also true for those who suffer from depression. I want to look at four scriptures that are often used to justify people's illness. All four are God's word, but Satan has twisted them into a lie to make them accept his oppression. I call these the 'four negative scriptures;' they are not really negative but people regularly use them in a negative way.

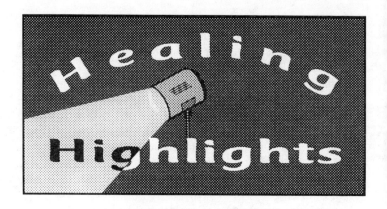

The Harling Family

Ben was God's special gift to the Harling family. But while he was still a baby it was clear that something was wrong. During the first year of his life Mr. and Mrs. Harling discovered that Ben was unable to tolerate certain foods. Wrong foods would cause a change

in their little boy's behaviour and he was also very sick. By the time his first birthday came, they had a long list of forbidden food, which included fish, apples, nuts, and all dairy products. When Ben ate something 'forbidden,' the whole family would suffer for 36 hours as he became hyperactive and sick.

A dietician at the local hospital was amazed at just how many foods were causing Ben to react. She had no help to offer; neither had their G.P. until he finally referred Ben to an Ear, Nose and Throat consultant. He diagnosed a food intolerance caused by a leaky gut lining, which has the same symptoms as food allergies.

As the doctors advised the Harlings about Ben, it became obvious that problems other members of the family suffered from, were also related to similar types of complaint. The result was that to varying degrees the family were all restricted to certain foods.

In 1989 Don held an Autumn Tour meeting, near to the Harling's home. The entire Harling family (John & Alison and four children) went for the team to pray for them. Alison writes 'the "diagnosis" was a spirit of infirmity affecting the family. The spirit was cast out by the authority of the Lord Jesus and since then Ben has never looked back.

The next day we tested Ben to see what God had done. We gave him some "forbidden" food to eat and there was no reaction! He had a different one every day until we couldn't think of any more. Then the other members of the family started to work through their lists too. The release was wonderful. Gradually, over a matter of weeks we found that all of the forbidden foods were now OK and by Christmas, Ben could eat normally and his grandmother commented on how well behaved he was over Christmas.'

Ben's father, John, wrote to Don and said, 'Since then the only times we experienced anything like the old problems were when Ben ate something with artificial colouring, or when he was ill, with a cold for instance. Fifteen months later even these remaining problems have disappeared. The rest of the family are also enjoying the blessings of freedom from that spirit of infirmity.'

The famous four are Job's boils, Timothy's stomach, Trophimus's sickness, and Paul's thorn. I find that many Christians know more about these four things than they know of the promises of God to heal them in rest of the Bible.

Job's Boils

'And the LORD restored Job's losses when he prayed for his friends. Indeed the LORD gave Job twice as much as he had before.' (Job 42:10)

The story of Job is one that touches deep issues. Job's suffering and the conversations he had with his 'friends' are well known but very misunderstood. Job was afflicted with boils, sores that broke out all over his skin. Before the boils appeared he had lost all his possessions, flocks of sheep and camels and his children. The only thing he didn't lose was his wife, which wasn't necessarily a blessing because even she advised Job to *'Curse God and die!'* (Job 2:9).

In the King James Version of the Bible verse 10 of Chapter 42 says *'the Lord turned the captivity of Job, when he prayed for his friends.'* That strikes a chord with many people, sickness is a captivity. When I am ill I feel I am in prison, I am restricted in what I can do.

On one visit to Zimbabwe I went down with a stomach 'bug.' I was so ill I could not move for an hour or two; this was not a blessing. It was not even comfortable to lie in bed. We had a five hundred kilometre car journey to get to the next crusade and I wanted to be up and on my way. The sickness held me captive and it got me frustrated and feeling low. Eventually, Heather, my wife, with one of the brothers on my team said, 'Come on, we are leaving. We are going to get you up in faith.' They put me in the car still feeling very ill, but as soon as it was started, I was healed! Their faith was the channel for God's healing that freed me from my prison.

Historians tell us that the account of Job covers a maximum period of twelve months in the Bible. That means that in the space of twelve months Job lost his wealth and children, became sick **and** was healed. Many people talk about the patience of Job and the trials of Job which are fine but don't take them out of context. Job was not a long term sufferer. The important thing to note is that Job got healed and finished with twice as much as when he started.

If you feel that the story of Job describes your experience, make sure that you relate to the whole story. You can lose everything, you can be sick, but you will be healed and finish up with twice as much as you had before. Job's boils did not last a long time, there was an end to his suffering. So if Job is your model, be full of hope, the end is in sight!

Timothy's Stomach

'No longer drink only water, but use a little wine for your stomach's sake and your frequent infirmities.'
(1 Timothy 5:23)

It would appear that Timothy was often ill, his stomach being the cause of his ailments. From the tone of Paul's letter I guess it was a cause of frustration, because it hampered the work Timothy had been called to do. I often meet people who are the same, frequently off work, or not in church meetings because of 'bugs.'

Paul's advice was don't drink only water, take some wine as well. For Timothy the bugs he got probably came from the water he drank; wine did, and still does have some healing benefit. Paul was saying to Timothy, 'You have a weak stomach, I want you to get healed from it. The water you drink is not healthy, drink some wine and live healthily.' His motivation was to bring about an improvement in Timothy's health. If you suffer with a complaint like Timothy's, note that Paul is not saying drink a little wine so you can put up with a bad stomach, rather drink a little wine and be healed. I am confident that Paul knew it was God's will for Timothy to be healed, and not hampered by continual 'bugs.'

Trophimas' Sickness

'Erastus stayed in Corinth, but Trophimus I have left in Miletus sick.' (2 Timothy 4:20). It's only a passing reference to this man and not much information, but some people have built a whole theory that it's not God's will to heal everyone, from this one verse. Is their conclusion about God's will, correct? What is behind Paul's comment?

I'm sure that Trophimus was left in Miletus to recover, to convalesce. It's possible that he had the same problem as Epaphroditus who is mentioned in Philippians 2:

> *'Yet I considered it necessary to send to you Epaphroditus, my brother, fellow worker, and fellow soldier, but your messenger and the one who ministered to my need; since he was longing for you all, and was distressed because you had heard that he was sick. For indeed he was sick almost unto death; but God had mercy on him, and not only on him but on me also, lest I should have sorrow upon sorrow. Therefore I sent him the more eagerly, that when you see him again you may rejoice, and I may be less sorrowful. Receive him therefore in the Lord with all gladness, and hold such men in esteem; because for the work of Christ he came close to death, not regarding his life, to supply what was lacking in your service toward me.'*
>
> (Philippians 2:25–30)

In his work for the Gospel, Epaphroditus had fallen sick and almost died. I believe his illness was stress and overwork; the demands of preaching and teaching had been so great he had neglected to rest properly. The result was what some would call 'burn-out,' or 'breakdown.' Just think about the practical demands of a ministry planting new churches in all the major cities of the known world. I am sure that all of Paul's co-workers had more than enough to do and some went too far. In their zeal for the Gospel, Epaphroditus, and possibly Trophimus, did too much without resting, and so got exhausted.

Things haven't changed that much in two thousand years of church history. Many servants of God still get sick through over-work and not allowing time for their bodies to rest. They tell me that it is a medical fact that preaching energetically for 45 minutes takes as much energy out of a person as six hours manual labour! So someone preaching and teaching, like the early church workers, every day for many days will burn up a lot of energy and can become ill.

I learnt the principle of resting the hard way; I had just arrived at a church, having flown from Belfast where we had preached and seen God move in marvellous ways. During the flight I felt ill, so ill that I thought I couldn't go on. Before the meeting started, I asked the minister to pray for me, but as he did he suddenly stopped and said, 'Don, the Lord tells me I have to rebuke you. You have to repent, because you are only suffering from over work. The reason for feeling as you do is that you have been doing too much and not resting.'

Of course, the Lord was right. I accepted that Word of Knowledge, and asked the Lord for forgiveness. The minister prayed and I was healed. However, that was not the end, because I had to produce the fruit of repentance which meant in this case giving time for rest. (Read the chapter on Healthy Living for more on this.)

So Trophimus and Epaphroditus needed to recover. For Epaphroditus, his healing was not a supernatural miracle, he just needed some time to rest. If you think you are like Trophimus, then get your diary and make time to rest.

Paul's Thorn

Of the four scriptures that are misused this one is most often used as an excuse for not being healed. It makes me sad that so many people accept their sickness, describing it as their 'thorn in the flesh.' They convince themselves that it may not be God's will to have the 'thorn' removed, when the truth is that God wants to heal them.

Most Christians seem to have their own theory of what the thorn was. I have heard preachers trying to prove it was everything from a hunchback to an eye disease, and even an unconverted mother-in-law or wife! Peter warns us against pet theories (2 Peter 1:20) and it is always very dangerous to take one verse out of its context. So, what does Paul actually say?

'And lest I should be exalted above measure by the abundance of the revelations, a thorn in the flesh was given to me, a messenger of Satan to buffet me, lest I be exalted above measure. Concerning this thing I pleaded with the Lord three times that it might depart from me. And He said to me, "My grace is sufficient for you, for My strength is made perfect in weakness." Therefore most gladly I will rather boast in my infirmities, that the power of Christ may rest upon me. Therefore I take pleasure in infirmities, in reproaches, in needs, in persecutions, in distresses, for Christ's sake. For when I am weak, then I am strong.'

(2 Corinthians 12:7–10)

What was Paul's thorn in the flesh? It was *'a messenger of Satan to buffet [him].'* Note that it came from the devil, **not** from God. Why did he have it? Because he had an abundance of revelation (v7). If you think you have a thorn, fine, but I have one question, what is the revelation you have had? To qualify for a thorn in the flesh you need to have the abundance of revelation to go with it! There is a sense in which I wish a few more of the people who said they have thorns really did, because the Church is in real need of the type of revelation Paul had!

If you look in the preceding chapter there is an indication of what Paul thought the thorn was.

'Are they ministers of Christ? I speak as a fool; I am more: in labors more abundant, in stripes above measure, in prisons more frequently, in deaths often. From the Jews five times I received forty stripes minus one. Three times I was beaten with rods; once I was stoned; three times I was shipwrecked; a night and a day I have been in the deep; in journeys often, in perils of waters, in perils of robbers, in

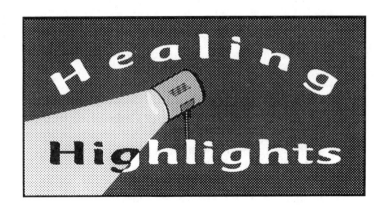

Stephen Chu

During an Autumn Tour meeting in 1985 Don Double had a word of knowledge for someone who was deaf in the left ear. Stephen responded and went forward so that Don could pray for him. God opened his deaf ear so that he could hear the faintest whisper.

It wasn't until after the meeting that the team discovered why he was deaf. As a child Stephen had an operation which removed all the bones in his left ear. He explained that it is those bones that enable us to hear, thus after the operation he was totally deaf in that ear. We are unsure what happened medically, but what was certain was Stephen could hear. What loving Father our God is!

perils of my own countrymen, in perils of the Gentiles, in perils in the city, in perils in the wilderness, in perils in the sea, in perils among false brethren; in weariness and toil, in sleeplessness often, in hunger and thirst, in fastings often, in cold and nakedness; besides the other things, what comes upon me daily: my deep concern for all the churches.' (2 Corinthians 11:23–28)

That is Paul's thorn in the flesh and the rest of the Bible confirms that. A thorn in the side is never used to describe sickness, it is always to do with persecution, e.g. Numbers 33:55; Joshua 23:13; Ezekiel 28:24. One thing Paul could always guarantee was that everywhere he went he would see revival and persecution.

In verse 8 of chapter 12 Paul said he prayed three times for the Lord to take the thorn away; I don't think I could have stopped praying after three times! Paul had such grace in God that he could stop and accept that persecution was part of his call. In the days after his conversion, Paul says the Lord showed him what was ahead. He was shown the things he was to suffer for the name of Christ. Yet he still accepted Jesus Christ as his personal saviour. When Paul faced God, he was presented with a future of blessing and persecution. The two things went together, and it was to be no 'bed of roses' for Paul.

Too much evangelism today presents the Christian life in the opposite way. We need to present Jesus Christ as Lord. One of the outcomes of true repentance should be that our lives come under the rule and reign of the Lord Jesus Christ. If you thought Paul's thorn was a sickness and perhaps you had a similar one, take God's word in its context. Do not make words mean something else; accept the correction of God's Word and see that you can be healed.

Chapter 7

Positives that Destroy Negatives – I

By now you will have seen that I view healing as a very positive thing. God wants to bless us, to make us whole. However there are negatives involved in healing which we must not ignore and in the next two chapters I want to look at some of the negative things that stop people being healed; we will then look at God's positive answers that destroy the negatives.

The negative things we are going to look at can prevent us enjoying the full healing God has for us. Sadly, I find that many people allow these negative things to control them. They want to be healed but their prayers don't seem to get answered. Let me give you a wonderful key to receiving your healing. If you have asked God to heal you, and you are still ill, ask Him why. Simple, isn't it? Be honest with God.

Has God said something to you which you have ignored or not done anything about? If, after asking God 'Why am I not healed?' it appears that heaven is silent, the best thing to do, is to go back to the last thing that God said. Take a few moments to reflect on what God has been saying to you; have you done what He asked? If not, the truth is that He does not have anything else to say, until you are moving in what He has already said.

Having made sure we're living in obedience to God, let's look at some of the reasons why people don't get healed. These are many and varied but here are five possible causes.

1. Reputation

Are you looking for God to heal you? Of course your answer will be yes, but check your thinking. Many people are running after someone with a reputation as a healer.

Most ministers who see God heal people in their meetings face this problem. All it needs is one extraordinary miracle, which gets publicised, and that man is in demand as 'a Healer.' Then he gets a following of people, most of them expecting him to heal them. I can guarantee one thing, they will always be disappointed. That is a point Satan gets in with his lies: 'So and so was healed because they are favoured. God's forgotten you. You are not good enough, you can't be healed.' Those are roots of unbelief and doubt, so be careful; don't run after people with reputations, run after Jesus.

The Apostles had the same problem. In Acts 3 we read Peter said,

> *'Silver and gold I do not have, but what I do have I give you: In the name of Jesus Christ of Nazareth, rise up and walk. And he took him by the right hand and lifted him up, and immediately his feet and ankle bones received strength ... Now as the lame man who was healed held on to Peter and John, all the people ran together to them ... greatly amazed. So when Peter saw it, he responded to the people: "Men of Israel, why do you marvel at this? Or why look so intently at us, as though by our own power or godliness we had made this man walk?"'* (Acts 3:6–7; 11–12)

Peter was very aware of the truth that even the faith for healing comes out of a relationship with Jesus. It comes down to us from God and we release it back up to Him and get healed.

Too often we take our eyes off Jesus and put it on the 'gifted' man. The truth is that Jesus gives the gift, through the Holy Spirit, from the Father. I like the idea that we are just the hose-pipe through which the living water is delivered. A garden hose is only useful whilst water comes out, to take the water to the right place. We need to keep our eyes on Jesus, the Living Water, and note what Philippians 2:7 says about His reputation:

> 'But [He] made himself of no reputation, taking the form of a bondservant and coming in the likeness of men.'

Jesus deliberately avoided the 'fan club' image. After healing several people, the Gospels record that He told them to keep quiet about what happened; of course, they told everybody that Jesus had healed them. This did not matter because what Jesus was doing was making himself of no reputation. He came to be a servant and if he met sick folk his first attitude was to get them healed.

The secret to healing is not the reputation of a man but the anointing. Acts 10:38 says, 'God anointed Jesus with the Holy Spirit and with power, who went about doing good and healing all who were oppressed by the devil: for God was with Him.' The anointing of God will set you free. If you see it on a man's ministry, great; the anointing of God will finish the sickness and disease in your life. Make sure that all the glory for the healing goes to God.

Back in the fifties there was a man called Jack Coe who saw some amazing miracles of healing in his services. One day a woman in a wheelchair was brought to him and he prayed for her but nothing happened. As he went on to the next person, he heard her say to herself, 'Now I've tried them all! I've tried 'X' and 'Y' and 'Z' and nothing happened; now I have tried this fellow Coe and nothing has happened again.' Jack Coe went back to her, looked her in the eyes and said, 'You hypocrite! You need to repent, it's Jesus alone that heals.' So she went home and she spent the night in prayer and repented of her sin. The next day she went back for Jack to pray for her. As he prayed the wheelchair went one way, and she went running in the other direction, completely whole. The difference was who she looked to for healing; when she got that right everything changed.

2. No Point of Contact

I believe people often miss healing because they have no fixed point of contact. They come very hopefully, but with a 'what will be, will be' attitude. When you look at the scriptures, at the people God healed, the opposite is usually true. They knew they were going to be healed, they released their faith and went to Jesus knowing what was going to happen.

The best example is one we've already looked at (see chapter 1) and I want to go back to the story of the woman with the issue of blood because there are more lessons we can learn. (Read Mark 5:24–34 for her story.) The woman had been ill for twelve years; the Bible says she suffered a great deal under the care of many doctors and had spent all her savings. After twelve years she realised that she was no better, and was getting worse.

Maybe you are like that; you've tried so hard to get healed, but are at the place where things are only getting worse. I call that place 'Wits End Corner.' At the point when you say, 'That's it, there is nothing more I can do,' God will speak. You will hear a voice whispering in your ear, 'But now I can do something.' God specialises in taking over in situations like that, because there is nothing too hard for the Lord.

After twelve long years this woman heard about Jesus. Have you heard about Him? That may seem a silly question, but have you heard that Jesus can heal the kind of physical or emotional condition that you have got? Do you believe that He really can heal your sickness? For God there is no difference between healing headaches or AIDS. It takes the same amount of power to heal them. He can do it.

The next step is to put that belief to use. When she heard about Jesus the woman settled how she was going to get healed. She set a point of contact – she began to say within herself, 'if I touch His clothes I will be healed.' This is an important lesson. Until your thinking is right, any external actions won't work; 'I'll wait and see what happens,' doesn't work. The woman made her mind up that she would be healed. Her determination and faith were rewarded. I can see her walking down the street saying 'When I touch the hem of

His garment, I shall be healed. He might not even see me, but it does not matter whether he sees me or not, I am going to touch the hem of His garment. I am going to get healed.' What's your thinking like? Have you decided you are going to be healed?

Once you have decided what is going to happen, what you use as a point of contact isn't important. Whatever it is, remember that it does not have any magical properties. Your point of contact only acts as the release for your faith. In Acts we read of handkerchiefs being used, and I've heard of all sorts of things being used, including squares of canvas from old marquees! What you touch physically is unimportant. Your faith has got to reach beyond that and touch Jesus. This is what happened for the lady, she touched a piece of cloth that Jesus was wearing. It was no different to the clothing you are wearing now, just an ordinary piece of fabric. But her faith went beyond that, touched Jesus and drew out from Him the virtue that healed her.

Once you settle in your heart the point of contact, whether it is a man praying or you touching a piece of cloth, you can pray in faith. At the moment you pray, Jesus responds to your faith.

3. Unbelief

Unbelief is a common thing; it stops many people from enjoying health. It is different from what we have been looking at in the last section, because it is a stronger feeling. Unbelief is the thought that 'God can't, or won't, heal me.'

When Jesus went to Nazareth, *'He could do no mighty work there, except that He laid His hands on a few sick people and healed them.'* (Mark 6:5) The next verse gives the reason, *'And He marvelled because of their unbelief.'* That is still true today, unbelief will hinder healing.

In Romans 14:23 we read, *'For whatever is not from faith is sin.'* Don't call unbelief 'lack of faith,' the Bible calls it Sin. How do you deal with sin? Simple – repent. Repenting of sin means to take responsibility for it, confess it to God and accept forgiveness and turn your back on the unbelief.

You cannot repent unless you take responsibility; it's always the first sign of true repentance. Refusing to take responsibility is something that goes right back to the Garden of Eden, and its modern manifestation is the P.O.M.s – the Poor Old Me syndrome. Find someone who is depressed, with a big dose of the P.O.M.s and you will find that last thing they ever want to do is to take responsibility. It is exactly what Adam did.

God came to Adam and asked what was going on. Adam said it was the woman's fault, and also blamed God for giving her to him. When God asked Eve the same question she blamed the serpent. It's our sinful nature to blame someone else for our condition. The truth is that the way to get healed and delivered is first to take responsibility and then start repenting. It is so easy to blame someone else, but until you take responsibility, you will probably stay sick for the rest of your life.

Repentance is a very positive word. It is a word of healing, of wholeness, blessing, and of progress. Repentance is not negative nor is it old fashioned.

'Therefore I say to you, whatever things you ask when you pray, believe that you receive them, and you will have them.' (Mark 11:24). This is a very difficult thing to do. Jesus made a promise here – when you pray, believe that your prayer has been heard. Receive the answer in faith, and look for its arrival. When it comes to healing this can be a dangerous area because some people get into 'mind over matter.' Trying to believe yourself well doesn't involve Jesus and so is wrong.

People ask, 'How will I know I am healed? Is it when the pain goes?' My answer is always the same, 'Believe, receive your healing by faith.' As the woman touched Jesus she knew she had got her answer. He was unaware that she was touching him in the natural sense, but the moment her faith touched that piece of cloth it drew virtue, healing power, out of Jesus, and He knew about it. Somebody had taken something that He was willing to give.

When you ask for prayer, do the same as this lady. Believe and receive your healing. The symptoms may not change immediately but don't be discouraged. I always encourage

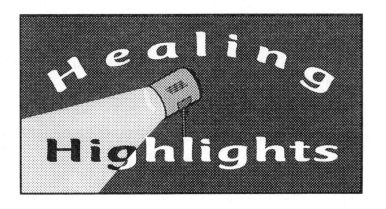

Blodwen Jones

For 69 years Blodwen Jones wore plaster supports and a leather jacket to keep her back straight. She suffered with osteoarthritis in her spine, shoulders and knees. This had been caused when, aged 11, she had been involved in an accident and a spike went through her back and damaged her spine. Blodwen says of the photo shown here, 'I was in such terrible agony. I'd just been to the orthopaedic clinic and had a double plaster taken off and a leather jacket put on in its place. Everytime I see this photo I remember the years of terrible suffering, but **now** I'm **free**.'

During a mission Don was holding in Corwen, North Wales, Blodwen went forward for prayer. As Don and the team prayed, Jesus touched her. The osteoarthritis went, and Blodwen was free. Two years later she says 'I feel 40 instead of 80. I saw my doctor recently, and he is still amazed that I have no pain. He has had to accept that I am healed, because of the wonderful peace God has given me.'

people to do the following when I pray for them; believe, receive by exercising faith, and then praise. It's polite to say thank you for a gift! As you thank God don't go to your body to see if the pain has gone or not. Believe the facts. If you have fixed your point of contact, and believe God's promise of healing, you are on scriptural grounds. You can be healed. Express your praise to God. Here is the fine line between unbelief and faith. Unbelief looks to see if the pain is still there and faith looks to the Healer.

4. The Occult

Any kind of involvement with the occult will be a hindrance to receiving God's blessing. You might think that is a very sweeping statement, but it's true.

One vivid example I remember was in a big church in Chicago, in the U.S. After I had preached, I invited folk to come forward to be filled with the Holy Spirit. As we prayed, there was a teenage girl, who was having problems receiving the Holy Spirit, and nothing was happening. As I began to pray for her, the Lord said, 'She's been involved in the occult.' I asked her about this and she told me that she read her horoscopes and had had her fortune told. When I showed her that this was wrong, she confessed and repented of the sin. We then cut off the effect of the occult and without going any further she started speaking in tongues. In other words she could not get filled with the Holy Spirit until she got the problem out of the way. It is the same with healing, the occult does stop healing taking place.

At this point many people say 'I don't believe in the occult. It doesn't affect me and I only read the horoscopes for fun.' Horoscopes are not harmless fun. As you read them you are planting seed. How? When you read the Word of God, you put the seed of the Word in your heart, it's watered by the Spirit and it springs forth and yields fruit after a time. When you read a horoscope the same happens, only this time you are reading the word of the devil. You plant his seed in your heart; the fruit is a 'dry' heart, one that is closed to the Holy Spirit and that always means bondage.

The Bible makes it very clear what God thinks about occult activities. In Deuteronomy 18:10–11 there is a list, which helps us understand what is meant by the Occult. It includes the following which are all 'banned' activities: talking to a Spiritist or a Medium; being involved in black magic and witchcraft (I also include reading books about those kind of things); and divination, which today includes playing with the Ouija board or Tarot Cards, reading tea leaves and palmistry. God has banned all these things; the Bible calls them an abomination. If you have been involved in any of the above, you need to repent; you may have been unaware of God's commands but you still need to be delivered. By taking responsibility and confessing your sin, God will bring healing to you. Read Deuteronomy 18:9–22 and see what God has to say to you about it.

5. Independence

The fifth thing I want us to look at is the sin of independence. Some folk will never get healed because they are too independent. Adam and Eve acted independently of God. God had said, '*You shall not,*' but they did.

When we get right with God, one of the first things to change is we learn to be dependent on God. Jesus is our perfect example, He said that without God He could do nothing (John 5:19). The Amplified Bible really captures Jesus' attitude, '*I am able to do nothing from Myself – independently, of my own accord – but as I am taught by God and as I get His orders. I decide as I am bidden to decide. As the voice comes to Me, so I give a decision.*' (John 5:30 Amplified).

Jesus spent His whole life on this earth doing exactly what His Father showed Him; He was utterly dependent on His Father. If Jesus needed to be dependent on His Father, you and I need to be dependent on Him as well.

God has put us in a Body, or in a family, the family of God. You might not like it but you need other people. We need one another. Have you ever tried to pray through to get healed by

May Wright

'I praise the Lord because He has healed me. For almost thirty years I had suffered with osteoarthritis of the spine, the neck, in my knees and hands; in fact it was in most of my joints. I wore a surgical corset and had been on medication for several years. Due to swelling and pain in my right hand I found it difficult to knit and sew and was unable to easily walk up or down stairs because of the pain in my knee joints.

On November 15th 1990 my daughter took me to Don's meeting at Ipswich. I went forward for healing and was prayed for with hands laid on me. The Lord Jesus touched me and I felt wonderful! I was able to bend down and touch my toes, and praise God I was able to touch them. When I went back to my seat the swelling in my fingers had disappeared and they were straight and free from pain. Since that day I have not taken any medication because I am so well.

I have told my doctor that I do not need any more pills because God has completely healed me. I feel a different person, free from pain and able to do things I have not done for years. My friends are amazed at my transformation.

I want to praise and thank God that at the age of seventy one He has restored me and made me whole again.'

yourself and it hasn't been answered? Why didn't God answer your prayer? If you have an independent spirit that is probably the reason.

When I meet people who are sick I usually ask them, 'Have you been prayed for?' If they say no, then I will offer to pray because Jesus' attitude was to always minister to the sick people He met. Very occasionally I meet someone who says 'No thank you. I will pray for myself.' That is independence. God has put us together in the Body because we need each other, and the life that flows from one part of the Body to another.

As you have read this chapter you may have recognised things that you now realise were preventing your healing. Don't be disheartened, in the next chapter we will look at God's positives which will destroy these negatives.

Chapter 8

Positives that Destroy Negatives – II

In the last chapter we saw that going after a man with a reputation, not having a point of contact, unbelief, involvement in the occult and independence can all stop people being healed. Now I want to show you God's answer to these negatives.

> *'Is anyone among you suffering? Let him pray. Is anyone cheerful? Let him sing psalms. Is anyone among you sick? Let him call for the elders of the church, and let them pray over him, anointing him with oil in the name of the Lord. And the prayer of faith will save the sick, and the Lord will raise him up. And if he has committed sins, he will be forgiven. Confess your trespasses to one another, and pray for one another, that you may be healed. The effective, fervent prayer of a righteous man avails much.'*
>
> (James 5:13–16)

Is anyone suffering? The Translator's New Testament says *'Is anyone of you troubled?'* whilst the Amplified Bible puts it this way, *'Is any one among you afflicted – ill treated, suffering evil? He should pray.'* James is known as a blunt writer, he doesn't waste words. He says, 'if you are suffering, the answer is simple, pray about it.'

I looked in Webster's dictionary to find out what the word 'troubled' really meant. He says 'troubled' means disordered, agitated mentally or spiritually, stressed or uncertain of mind, worried, oppressed, in physical disorder, to put into confused motion, disarranged. If you are sick does this definition describe your symptoms? James instructed us that if anyone is like that, let them pray. Perhaps prayer is the last thing a person wants to do when they are bound by those kind of things, but the instruction is very clear – when you are in that condition, pray.

He goes on to say that if anyone is feeling cheerful then he should sing praises to God. Recently as I was studying this chapter of James, I looked at the second part of verse thirteen in several translations of the Scriptures and this is what I found. *'Is any one merry?'* (King James Version); *'Is any one in good spirits?'* (The New Testament in Modern Speech, R.F. Weymouth); *'Is any one in a happy mood?'* (The New Testament: A Translation in the language of the People, C.B. Williams); *'Is any one in a good heart?'* (New English Bible), and to all of these people James says they should sing psalms and praises to God.

As I read these different versions I wondered if the reason why many of us are sick is that we wrongly use our joy, our happiness and our good moods. I believe His praise should continually be in my mouth; if my mouth is full of praise it's full of something positive and good, and it's making a highway for God into my life. Making a highway for God allows no room for the devil's landing strips, which can be the source of sickness in my body. So, ask yourself this question, 'Are you sometimes troubled and ill treated and suffering because when you are happy and glad you have not expressed it to the Lord in singing to Him?'

The Positive of Encouragement

As I've said, expressing joy in praise to God is an important key to staying whole. King Solomon in his book of Proverbs says the same thing several times.

> *'A merry heart makes a cheerful countenance, but by sorrow of the heart the spirit is broken.'* (Proverbs 15:13)

'The spirit of a man will sustain him in sickness, but who can bear a broken spirit?' (Proverbs 18:14)

'A merry heart does good, like medicine, but a broken spirit dries the bones.' (Proverbs 17:22)

We saw in an earlier chapter, that according to some doctors, one of the major causes of arthritis and its associated diseases is bitterness and resentment, or in the words of Solomon a broken spirit. It is interesting that Solomon, when he wrote the book of Proverbs more than 2,500 years ago, discovered a cause of a major sickness in our day.

'Anxiety in the heart of man causes depression, but a good word makes it glad.' (Proverbs 12:25). Do you ever find that when you are feeling 'down,' if someone comes along and says something positive to you, suddenly you begin to feel glad and you're released? The ministry of encouragement is very special and those who have got a ministry of encouragement do a very important job in the Body of Christ.

Encouragement is a God-given positive that will deal with some of the negatives that stop people being healed. I love to give people a little word of encouragement and to watch how God blesses them. Often when I do, their face begins to shine, and they begin to express something of the purpose of God in their lives; God's purpose for everyone of us is to live full of joy, praising Him.

Barnabas was known as an encourager. It was obviously so much part of his life that the church changed his name from Joseph to Barnabas, which means son of encouragement (Acts 4:36). Mary's cousin Elizabeth was a great encourager too. Read Luke 1:39–56 and notice Elizabeth's response to Mary's news; pure encouragement. She could have reacted with doubt and unbelief, which would have done Mary no good, but instead Elizabeth chose to encourage.

When was the last time you encouraged someone? Remember that what you sow is what you will reap. If you are not being encouraged you ought to change what you are sowing, and deliberately make a point of encouraging some of the people around you. A good word makes us glad. That's healing, and is a pleasant medicine.

Do you realise that we can bring healing to people, by simply speaking good words of encouragement? Joy is a great healer, *'a merry heart does good, like medicine.'* (Proverbs 17:22). *'The joy of the LORD is your strength.'* (Nehemiah 8:10). Releasing the joy of the Lord will produce strong, victorious, healthy Christians. Suppressing the joy produces weak, defeated Christians. I once heard someone say that a Christian without joy is like Samson with a haircut! So be full of Jesus' joy.

> *'Is anyone among you sick? Let him call for the elders of the church, and let them pray over him, anointing him with oil in the name of the Lord.'* (James 5:14)

Why is it that at times there seem to be more sick people in the Church than there are in the world? The Church should be a barracks for the army of God, rather than a hospital for the sick. I am convinced that it is time that Church set a goal to get to the place where it didn't have any sick people because they have all been healed.

James makes it very clear what should we should do if we are sick. He puts a responsibility on sick people not to stay sick; they are to call for the elders of the Church. I take that to mean that if you are ill you should call for the elders of the Church before you call for the doctor. It saddens me that people will only look for prayer to be healed, after the doctor's treatment has failed. There is a lesson in the book of 2 Chronicles that we need to pay attention to: *'And in the thirty-ninth year of his reign, Asa became diseased in his feet, and his malady was very severe; yet in his disease he did not seek the LORD, but the physicians. So Asa rested with his fathers; he died in the forty-first year of his reign.'* (2 Chronicles 16:12–13) Asa, like many of us, turned to the doctor rather than turning to God first. The result was that within two years he was dead. Maybe King Asa would have had a longer reign if he had sought God first when he became ill.

Gwynneth Wilmott

'About ten years ago your crusade came to the field by the Health Centre at Portishead, Bristol. I was on my way to see my doctor and noticed your tent. At the time I was being treated for depression and suicidal tendencies; it was termed "manic depression." The doctor was treating me with Lithium tablets, and periodically put me in hospital for more intensive treatment. I never liked taking the tablets because I felt that they stopped me thinking properly.

I didn't go into your tent, but the Lord touched me as I saw it. He touched my spirit; until I was seventeen I had been a church goer but had then stopped. I had always believed in God, but I had never known Him, like I have since the crusade, when He became my personal Lord.

Later in your crusade I went to a meeting and was healed of an emotional hurt, and I was then saved. I am no longer suicidal or depressed and I know how much my life has changed, since Jesus came and gave me new life. Since the crusade the Lord has been healing my emotions and attitudes.

Praise the Lord for the work He has, and continues to do, in me.'

The Positive Prayer of Faith

When the elders come and pray, they pray the prayer of Faith. The Lord told James to write those words, not because He wanted to mock us and withhold healing. **No**, God wants the elders to pray so that we can be healed. I want you to notice that it is a prayer of faith, not a prayer of 'I hope so,' or 'it might work,' or 'there's a chance it will happen.' The elders pray a prayer of **faith**. There's not a doubt in it.

I don't believe the prayer of faith is just saying the right words. If that were so we could take the words of some of the great healing ministries like Oral Roberts, Kathryn Kuhlman or Smith Wigglesworth, learn them off by heart and then just pray them over people. That's not the prayer of faith and it doesn't work. The prayer of faith is the prayer of authority. Again it is not just saying the right words because you could learn words of authority without the revelation of what authority is. Authority is to do with a person, Jesus.

In ancient times a person's name was not just a means of identification, it spoke of their authority and of their character. The prayer of faith is based on a revelation of the authority of Jesus and the character of His life on earth. Jesus lived on this earth for over 33 years and He never once sinned. He lived a perfect, righteous, holy life that was totally acceptable to God. That gives the name of Jesus authority. When Jesus triumphed over death and sat down at the right hand of the Father, He was given all authority in heaven and on earth. That is the authority which we move in, when we pray in faith and in Jesus' name.

The Roman centurion understood this about Jesus (Luke 7). My visits to Africa have taught me why the centurion was so affected by his servant's sickness. In many parts of the world people still have servants, who clean the house, do the washing and the ironing, and cook, clean the car and look after the garden. Can you imagine how that Roman soldier's family felt when their servant was sick? No wonder he went to Jesus for help!

The centurion sent a message to Jesus that his servant was sick and dying. The moment Jesus heard the word 'sick,' he

94

responded immediately; somehow that word 'sick' just moves Jesus. When the centurion heard Jesus was coming he sent a message to say, *'Lord, do not trouble Yourself ... say the word, and my servant will be healed'* (Luke 7:6–7).

When he said that it was clear he understood authority and what was happening when Jesus healed people. He said, *'For I also am a man placed under authority, having soldiers under me. And I say to one, "Go," and he goes; and to another, "Come," and he comes; and to my servant, "Do this," and he does it.'* (Luke 7:8). He recognised that Jesus was a man under authority and that was why what Jesus was doing worked.

Authority is about being 'under,' not being 'over.' Too many people try to heal the sick and cast out devils by shouting about the authority they have over the devil. The truth is that they need a revelation of whose authority they are under and whose authority they are using. I am what I am by the grace of God, because I'm submitted to Jesus and under His authority. If I'm not under His authority my words will not reach the ceiling, the devil will laugh and nothing will happen.

One of the hardest lessons I have had to learn in the ministry is that I don't have any authority just because it worked last time. I've tried that and fallen flat on my face. Only as I come in my personal, intimate relationship with Jesus, under authority, do I have any authority this time. If I'm not freshly under authority with Jesus, nothing happens.

A centurion had 100 soldiers under him, which is the equivalent of a sergeant in the British army. Having done National Service many years ago I know exactly what the authority of a centurion meant. I have never obeyed anybody, except Jesus, as I obeyed the officers in the army. If a sergeant told you to do something you did it, without any questions.

Why did the centurion have authority to command such obedience from his soldiers? Simply because he had a 'badge on his arm.' In the British Army, a sergeant has three stripes on his arm, and as a soldier if you see those three stripes, you don't argue. During my years in the army I was told to do some ridiculous things by officers, but I did them because of what their badge represented. The stripes meant that behind the speaker was a great deal of authority; for the centurion when he gave an order it was with the authority of Caesar, the greatest military and political power then on the earth. That badge said, 'What this man says, you do because it's the same as Caesar telling you to do it.'

When I stand to minister I wear a badge; I wear it on my forehead like the Old Testament priests. It says JESUS, and it's a badge of authority. It says I am under authority, and that when I speak it is as if Jesus were here saying the words Himself. That is a fearful thing and keeps my tongue holy, because I don't want to say things that Jesus would not say. To pray the prayer of faith we need to be in that position, under authority.

James then says the elders are to anoint with oil. What is the oil for? In the symbolism of the Bible, oil is often used to represent the Spirit of God. So to be anointed with oil is to experience the anointing of the Holy Spirit. My experience is that a church or a person without the moving and the anointing of the Holy Spirit is like a chicken sitting on a nest of eggs that have never been fertilised. Eventually they will go rotten! The anointing of the Holy Spirit is what brings life. When you are anointed with oil, James is saying that you are being anointed with the Holy Spirit.

Jesus lived for thirty years without the anointing; when He was baptised in the Jordan, the Bible says that the Holy Spirit came upon Him. In Luke 4 we read that He went into the wilderness full of the Spirit, and after forty days and the temptations of the devil, returned to Galilee in the power of the Spirit. He went into the temple, opened a scroll and read from Isaiah, *'The Spirit of the Lord is upon me, because He anointed me.'* From that moment on Jesus didn't just live a perfect life, He also lived a miracle life. Miracles flowed from Him wherever He went because of the anointing.

Jesus knew what that anointing was for: *'He has anointed Me to preach the gospel to the poor. He has sent Me to heal the brokenhearted, to preach deliverance to the captives and recovery of sight to the blind, to set at liberty those who are oppressed, to preach the acceptable year of the LORD.'* (Luke 4:18–19).

A word of caution, don't get confused between the anointing and adrenalin flowing. Some folk think that when the adrenalin is flowing the anointing is there. When Margaret Thatcher spoke she could get an audience 'hyped up,' very quickly. Whether you agree or disagree with her politics is not important, when she stood up to speak in the House of Commons, you could feel something happened. She could make you glad or mad, but she got the adrenalin going, but that was not anointing.

There's is also a difference between what we feel and the anointing of God. Some of the greatest times of anointing, and the greatest fruitfulness in my ministry have come when I didn't feel anything 'special'. Anointing with oil is just the outward symbol of what God is doing internally. Faith and the anointing have to function together.

> *'It shall come to pass in that day that his burden will be taken away from your shoulder, and his yoke from your neck, and the yoke will be destroyed because of the anointing oil.'*   (Isaiah 10:27)

We have got to get the anointing and the yoke together so that the yoke will be destroyed. In other words people will be set free from their afflictions as the anointing of the Holy Spirit comes upon them.

The Positive Joy of Confession

> *'Confess your trespasses to one another, and pray for one another, that you may be healed. The effective, fervent prayer of a righteous man avails much.'*   (James 5:16)

Confess your faults to one another and pray that you might be healed. Do you have any faults? Have you confessed them to somebody else? If not, maybe that is why you are sick. Confession is a good way to keep those independent attitudes dead; it is one way to grow humility.

For many people, the roots of the negatives we have looked

at are found in some deep emotional hurts. The hurts and wounds that get implanted in people's lives cause all sorts of reactions. As we have already seen an emotional reaction can result in all kinds of physical sickness. By using this positive key, confession, those hurts can be dealt with; let me illustrate with two personal testimonies.

When I was in my forties I discovered a hurt in my life that caused strong reactions. It showed itself in situations where I felt somebody was threatening me or something that I owned. I got angry, but inside there was an awful sense of rejection and insecurity. The problem was I did not have a clue where those feelings came from. One day I was talking this through with my colleague, Mike Darwood and he saw what it was.

When I was about five years old I caught tuberculosis. Back in those days it was almost incurable unless it was caught quickly, when with radical surgery there was hope; it was viewed very much like cancer is today. Before I was born my parents had a little girl who had only lived two weeks after birth, and so I was an only child. You can imagine what they felt when I was diagnosed as having TB.

I was rushed to hospital where someone, dressed in white who looked to me like a ghost, took me to the ward. That was the last I saw of my mother and father for a whole month, because parents were not allowed to visit their children in those days. My mother tells me that as she walked out of the hospital grounds they could still hear me screaming.

The emotional scar from that experience remained for a long time. Being taken away from Mum and Dad, and the wound of separation, had produced real insecurity. Mike prayed with me and the Spirit of God moved; the wound was healed and dealt with.

A few years ago I was invited to a church for a weekend of meetings; it was very fruitful and we had a great time. On the Monday morning, before we left, we had a short time of prayer with the leader of the church. This brother is very sensitive to the Holy Spirit and as we prayed he had a word of knowledge for me. He said, 'God has shown me there are two hooks in your heart.' What did that mean? God spoke through this brother and said that a Spirit of Control had got hold of me, two people had been controlling my life; it was to do with what was called 'heavy authority' and those kind of things. When you open yourself to wrong things a controlling spirit can get hold of you. Those hooks in my heart were affecting me, so I confessed it, the brother prayed for me, and I was delivered.

The point I am making is that I needed someone to pray for me. You need someone to pray for you. James 5:16 is clear, confess your faults one to another, pray for one another so that you might be healed. There is a whole wide range of emotional conditions, from the common depression to the deep, deep rejections, that need healing and the key is confession.

The Positive Fear of God

I want to finish this chapter with one further positive that is very, very important.

> 'Do not be wise in your own eyes; Fear the LORD and depart from evil. It will be health to your flesh, and strength to your bones.'   (Proverbs 3:7–8)

The Amplified Bible puts this verse in this way:

> 'Be not wise in your own eyes; reverently fear and worship the Lord, and turn [entirely] away from evil. It shall be health to your nerves and sinews, and marrow and moistening to your bones.'

The fear of the Lord will have a positive affect on your life. Other translations talk of the fear of God being *'nourishment to your bones,'* (the New Berkeley Version) and that *'This will mean health for your flesh and vigour for your bones.'* (New American Bible). I hope you've got the message!

The fear of the Lord is something that I believe God is trying to restore to the life of the Church; that we learn to fear and reverently respect Him. It is so important that the fear of God underpins everything in our lives. I fear God; I really do and the outcome of my fear is that I worship Him. Worship is not just singing choruses, worship is not just being in a meeting, worship is a lifestyle.

We can worship God all of the time. Worship is the expression of an intimate relationship with the Lord and it comes from acknowledging who He is and giving Him His rightful place in our lives. I don't want to live one tick of the clock when Jesus doesn't have His rightful place in my life. That's a very positive place to be because Jesus said He came to give us life: *'The thief does not come except to steal, and to kill, and to destroy. I have come that they may have life, and that they may have it more abundantly.'* (John 10:10). (If you want to read more about the positive affect of the fear of the Lord, get a copy of my book *The Positive Power of the Fear of God* published by Good News Crusade, 1990)

So, these are some of the positives that will deal with those negatives forces and attitudes that stop healing. If you want to be free from the negative apply the positive medicine of God's word, but note that they all involve an act of your will. You can choose to make use of God's provision for you; if you do, you will open the way for Him to heal you.

Chapter 9

Living a New Way

In Romania I heard a Baptist Pastor tell this true story:

> 'A man was taking his little daughter for a walk in the countryside. As they walked along the lane, he suddenly saw a beautiful insect, laying motionless on the ground in front of them. He motioned his daughter to be very still, and pointed out the insect to her. She was completely taken by it and stared in fascination for a long time. The girl and her father marvelled in its beauty, agreeing that it was a lovely creature. Suddenly, and without warning, the little girl lifted her foot and stamped hard on the insect, killing it. Her father was startled, and asked her why she had done that. She replied "It moved!"'

When something new happens that we have not experienced before, most people react in the same way. We say 'this is new, this is different; it cannot be right.' Human beings like the familiar, and a new idea or way of doing things can be unsettling. This can easily be followed by panic and a reaction to stop this new thing as soon as possible; 'control it before it takes control of us.'

During recent years the Holy Spirit has been moving in a mighty way. Wherever God's people have given Him the freedom to do so and have responded to His promptings, God has moved. Churches all over the country have introduced new ways of doing things; this is especially true in the area of healing. However, I have seen churches where the opposite has begun to happen. After a period of enjoying God's blessing, this freedom and openness to God has been withdrawn. As a result His work is hindered.

In the book of Job, God tells Job that He has fixed boundaries for the ocean. God says, *'This far you may come, but no farther, and here your proud waves must stop!'* (Job 38:11). It is right for God to speak thus to part of His creation, but it is not wise for a man to tell his Creator to stop! It is an awesome thing to put limits on how far we allow God to move in our lives and churches. As you have read this book, you may have discovered new ideas or ways to approach healing. If this is so, be careful what you do next.

When God delivered the Israelite nation out of Egypt, they obeyed Him and moved with Him. They followed the cloud by day and the pillar of fire by night. But in the desert they began to put limits on what they would do. The Bible says that they *'limited the Holy One of Israel.'* (Psalm 78:41). In spite of the mighty evidence they saw, they didn't believe that He was able to fulfil His plans for them. As a result of their unbelief a whole generation died in the desert and never entered the Promised Land. The Bible makes it clear that the way they limited God was in disobedience and unbelief. (Heb 3:16–19).

What a difference we see in the attitude of Billy Bray, the great Cornish evangelist. He declared that God is not limited and added that he belonged to the company called 'Father, Son and Holy Spirit Unlimited.' Because of his faith, God was able to use Billy in a time of revival in Cornwall. He built churches in the most unlikely places and without visible resources paid for them and saw them full to overflowing. Billy Bray was willing to give God room to move, and so God moved in Cornwall; God extended His Kingdom in an awe inspiring way.

It is a sobering fact that the only limits on God's Word are the ones we put on it. He has given us the freedom to either limit or release His power in our lives and churches! God did establish His people in the promised land of Canaan, but not with the generation that came out of Egypt. They spent forty years going round and round in the wilderness; the scale of this tragedy is evident when you realise that it only takes eleven days to walk from the Red Sea to the Promised Land. It was a lot easier to get the Children of Israel out of Egypt, than it was to get Egypt out of the Children of Israel!

One of the biggest hindrances to letting God have room to move in our lives is the traditions we establish. We easily form habits based on our experience of the way God has moved in the past. Sadly, it seems the more powerfully we have seen God move, the greater the barriers we erect against God ever doing things in a different way!

Our memories of past blessings prevent us from letting go of the old ways that we have established. We stop the Holy Spirit moving us on into something new and even better. It seems that we forget that God never wants to take us back into bondage or less productive ways. He always wants to move us on to better things and greater blessings.

In order to break out of and stay free from this bondage, it is helpful to remember Paul's words: *'forgetting those things which are behind.'* (Phil 3:13). This scripture is often applied to bad and negative things. From the context we can conclude that it may be more important that we break free from good things that are holding us back. I have found that the Good is often the enemy of the Best! God wants His children to have the best and that means letting the Holy Spirit take us to where we have never been before.

When the Israelites were finally on the banks of the River Jordan and ready to cross into the Promised Land, Joshua addressed them. He told them to follow the priests who were carrying the Ark of the Covenant, which symbolised the presence of God, because they *'[had] not passed this way before.'* (Joshua 3:4). They were obedient, and followed the Ark along that new way and moved into the land flowing with milk and honey.

To move on with God we need to have a pioneering Spirit; to be willing to go boldly where no one has been before! Abraham sets us a perfect example: *'By faith Abraham obeyed when he was called to go out to the place which he would afterward receive as an inheritance. And he went out, not knowing where he was going.'* (Heb 11:8). One area that I believe that the Holy Spirit longs to lead us into is a new dimension of healing. He wants to give us a manifestation of His power that parallels and goes beyond the things we read of in the Acts of the Apostles. We are to move into the realm of miracles performed by Jesus Himself and greater (John 14:12).

Dare we believe that ordinary men and women like you and I will do that? Will we walk on water, or feed thousands with a few bread rolls and pilchards, or change water into wine, or raise the dead and even pay our taxes with coins we find in fishes' mouths? Most of these things have been happening recently, to Christians in many parts of the world, who have given God freedom to move in their lives.

Every miracle recorded in the New Testament will be seen again, before Jesus returns, by those who dare to believe; I am convinced of that truth. If you find this hard to believe, remember the words of the angel to Mary. He told her that God had chosen her to be the mother of Jesus: *'For with God nothing will be impossible.'* (Luke 1:37). Neither can we ignore the words of the Lord Jesus Christ himself: *'Most assuredly, I say to you, he who believes in Me, the works that I do he will do also; and greater works than these he will do, because I go to My Father.'* (John 14:12). I have heard many attempts to explain away this verse. People have said that it does not mean what it says or only applies to preaching the Gospel and not to the miracles. To those who dare to believe it, I am convinced that Jesus meant what He said, and that His words will be proved correct. Are you prepared to let Him do this in your life? Or is your reply, 'You can come so far and no further, Lord.'

The temptation to settle is strong. No doubt, some people feel that they have already made great progress in their lives and churches and that now it would be nice to settle down. 'It's time to leave the pioneering to someone else; to allow some of the younger ones to be "out at the front."' Perhaps it would be more comfortable for a time, and there is certainly less risk

Joanna O'Keefe

Joanna was unable to move her neck freely. If she moved her head quickly it caused severe stabs of pain down her back. This caused great problems in everyday living; driving in particular was a very painful activity. She had suffered with this stiff neck for several years, but in 1988 God changed everything.

At Good News Crusade's family camp at Malvern, Worcestershire the Lord healed her. Joanna says, 'it was instantly released, it had been so stiff and painful for years. I had been to a chiropractor for help but he hadn't done much. But God healed me completely; it has been three years and I've been free of pain, thank the Lord.'

involved; but is it really safe? I am certain that settlers are in greater risk than pioneers; it's too easy to get comfortable with the familiar things around us. Being comfortable will always produce drowsiness and cause some people to fall asleep spiritually. Then the sleeper is quite impotent, and useless to the Kingdom of God. We need to keep and develop that pioneering spirit.

All this is particularly true for those of us who are leaders in the Church. It is very easy to become the 'cork in the bottle.' How easy it is, like the little girl in the story, to put our foot down on any move of God, killing it before it has really started. Leaders have an awesome responsibility to ensure that God has room to move in the church. When I was beginning my ministry, someone told me to let the Holy Spirit loose in my meetings, and to be ready for anything to happen. I have found this to be an invaluable piece of advice over the past thirty years, as I have sought to give the Holy Spirit His rightful place in my ministry. My goal is to always let God do what He wants, when He wants, and however He wants.

The first two chapters of this book looked at the variety of methods Jesus used to heal people. John says at the end of his Gospel: *'And there are also many other things that Jesus did, which if they were written one by one, I suppose that even the world itself could not contain the books that would be written.'* (John 21:25). It's clear that the Gospels are really only the 'edited highlights,' and that Jesus healed many more people than are recorded in the Gospels. Therefore we need to be open to God to do something through us that is new, or unusual. As I said about Jesus healing the blind man, would you be prepared to spit in someone's face, if God said that was the way they were to be healed?

I am certain that before Jesus comes we are going to witness the greatest revival the world has ever seen. The harvest of souls into the Kingdom of Jesus will happen on a world-wide scale that will make past revivals look small in comparison. As the harvest comes in, many people will be saved by seeing signs, wonders and healing miracles that are quite exceptional.

Already in many of the less developed countries I visit there

106

is a responsiveness to God's miracle power, that means thousands of people are giving up false gods and idols, and following Jesus Christ. One estimate says that at least 78,000 people are being born again everyday around the world, and that figure is going up. We are living in exciting times, days in which we need to stay open and flexible to what God is doing.

We have to learn that just because something is different, it does not mean that it is wrong. Nor does it automatically mean that the new thing is right, and the old thing is wrong. Many of us find it difficult to cope with change and this can certainly be a hindrance to a new move of the Holy Spirit. We need to develop a pioneering spirit and an adventurous attitude; an approach to life that will allow us to move into new areas of experience that the Holy Spirit has prepared for us. Then we will be able to lead others and will no longer be 'corks in bottles,' but shoehorns to ease feet into new shoes!

Be careful not to hinder that work by denying God room to move. We must remember the lesson in the story of the little girl. She was fascinated by the beauty of the insect; a moment later the insect's movement turned its beauty into something strange and terrifying to her. Overcome by fear, she put her foot down and killed it. Many people say 'No' to God, and will not allow Him to have freedom to move, because they are apprehensive of what might happen if they say yes. It is equally disastrous to say, 'That looks beautiful in some other church, but it is not for me,' all through fear of the unknown. Notice that fear is the restricting factor, but the Bible reassures us that, *'perfect love casts out fear.'* (1 John 4:18).

Let us put our trust in God's unquestionable love and push back the boundaries of our faith, expecting God to lead us into new realms of revelation. Then the Holy Spirit will be free to work in us and bring us into all that God has for us.

Chapter 10

Faith in the Cross

So far we have looked at Jesus healing our bodies and our minds, but there is one area of healing still to consider. Our spirits need to be healed. I have stressed that when Jesus healed people He used many different ways to bring healing to them. But, spiritual healing is different – there is only one way to find wholeness, a way that every person has to follow. The Cross on which Jesus died is at the heart of this and all healing. We need to see and understand what the cross represents.

Many people wear the cross as a symbol of their faith. Some wear crucifixes showing Jesus dying, others prefer an empty cross declaring that His death was not the end. In the same way that the Star of David is used as a symbol for Israel and all things Jewish, so the Cross is used to represent Christianity. But, the cross of Calvary is far more than a symbol. Everything that God has given to us has come through the Cross; from the small daily blessings to the big miracles, they all come via Calvary. On the cross, God's Son took everything that we are, that we might become everything that He is.

This is a life giving truth, which we need in our lives. But it is important that we take the truth of what the cross means in all its fulness. For those who revere the crucifix, look past Jesus' death and remember His victory over death; those who prefer the empty cross, don't ever forget the suffering, agony, and brutality that Jesus suffered for you.

You may wonder why it had to be a cross. After all,

crucifixion is one of the most cruel forms of execution the sin-warped mind of man has ever invented. We even have the word 'excruciating,' which is based on the Latin word meaning to crucify.

Jesus gave us one reason, when He was talking to Nicodemus: *'And as Moses lifted up the serpent in the wilderness, even so must the Son of Man be lifted up, that whoever believes in Him should not perish but have eternal life.'* (John 3:14–15).

Jesus is talking about an incident that happened to the Israelites, as they walked around the desert for forty years.

> *'Then they journeyed from Mount Hor by the Way of the Red Sea, to go around the land of Edom; and the soul of the people became very discouraged on the way. And the people spoke against God and against Moses: "Why have you brought us up out of Egypt to die in the wilderness? For there is no food and no water, and our soul loathes this worthless bread." So the LORD sent fiery serpents among the people, and they bit the people; and many of the people of Israel died. Therefore the people came to Moses, and said, "We have sinned, for we have spoken against the LORD and against you; pray to the LORD that He take away the serpents from us." So Moses prayed for the people. Then the LORD said to Moses, "Make a fiery serpent, and set it on a pole; and it shall be that everyone who is bitten, when he looks at it, shall live." So Moses made a bronze serpent, and put it on a pole; and so it was, if a serpent had bitten anyone, when he looked at the bronze serpent, he lived.'* (Numbers 21:4–9)

It is worth noting that the 'worthless bread,' they were complaining about was the manna God miraculously provided for them each day!

God sent a plague of poisonous snakes into the Israelite camp and as a result many people died. However, He did provide a way of salvation, an escape from death. God told Moses to make a bronze replica of the snakes, put it on a pole, and lift it up high. If anyone who was bitten looked up at the bronze snake, they would be healed. Jesus explained to Nicodemus that in the same way the Son of Man must be lifted up; anyone who would look up at the Lord Jesus Christ, would be saved from the poison of sin and would live forever.

The Cross is the pivotal point of history and of our lives. I've already said that Jesus took everything that we are, so that we might receive everything that He is. What was it that Jesus took from us, and what did He give back to us? Let's look at a few scriptures:

> *'For as by one man's disobedience many were made sinners, so also by one Man's obedience many will be made righteous.'*   (Romans 5:19)

He took all your sin that you might be made righteous and holy in His sight; you can exchange your sin for His righteousness.

> *'For you know the grace of our Lord Jesus Christ, that though He was rich, yet for your sakes He became poor, that you through His poverty might become rich.'*
> (2 Corinthians 8:9)

Paul is talking about material things; so you may come to the Cross with your poverty and leave with His riches, which includes healing, Hallelujah!

> *'He is despised and rejected by men, a man of sorrows and acquainted with grief.'*   (Isaiah 53:3)

At the cross Jesus experienced utter rejection and grief, so that you can come and leave your own at His feet. You can leave with His wholeness and healing.

> *'He Himself took our infirmities and bore our sicknesses.'*
> (Matthew 8:17 quoting Isaiah 53:4)

The cross and the crucifixion of Jesus are at the centre of all

111

true healing. If any supernatural healing does not involve the Cross of Jesus Christ, it is not of God. Faith Healers, Mediums and other 'alternative' methods do not lift up the Cross of Jesus; they do not present Him as the answer to people's conditions.

> *'Who Himself bore our sins in His own body on the tree, that we, having died to sins, might live for righteousness; by whose stripes you were healed.'*
>
> (1 Peter 2:24 quoting Isaiah 53:5)

The Gospels record that Pilate ordered Jesus to be flogged. He was handed over to the Roman soldiers who tied him to a post in the courtyard of their barracks. They then used a whip made of several strips of leather, into which bits of stone and bone had been sewn. When the Jews flogged a person they hit him 39 times, but the Romans had no such rules. Many floggings were enough to kill their victim. By the time they had finished, most of the skin had been ripped from Jesus' back. Why do I record such detail? After nearly two thousand years of Christianity, religion has blurred over and sanitized the sheer brutality of what Jesus suffered. The 'stripes' were not a series of neat weal marks across Jesus' back; blood poured from Jesus' back so that we might be healed.

Jesus paid an enormous price so that we could enjoy healing. By His stripes you were healed. Confess it now, out loud, making it personal for you: 'By Your stripes I am healed.' Believe it and receive your healing.

I want you to notice that Peter says *'By His stripes you **were** healed.'* He uses the past tense, meaning that you have already been healed. Peter boldly declares that every person was really healed as Jesus hung on the cross at Calvary. On the cross God laid the sickness that is in your body, on His Son. He bore it nearly 2,000 years ago, so that by your faith in Him and His Word, you can enjoy the reality of healing today.

I believe we need a revelation of the Cross in our own spirits; out of that we release our faith in the Cross and the Son of God, who became a substitute for us. We need that release of faith towards the Cross; not a release of faith towards healing, but towards the Healer – there is a big difference.

The Bible says God has dealt to every man a measure of faith. (Romans 12:3). Now the question is, are you using your faith? Is it active? Faith without corresponding action is dead (James 2:17, 20, 26). God wants your faith to be alive and, in the context of healing, for it to bring healing and wholeness to you and others. What is it that causes faith to die, to stop the works that make faith live? From my experience it is a thing suffered by Christians all over the world – doubt.

'If we confess our sins, He is faithful and just to forgive us our sins and to cleanse us from all unrighteousness.' (1 John 1:9) Every time I prepare to preach or minister I always go to God and ask Him to cleanse me from sin, by the blood of Jesus. Usually I will specifically name doubt as a sin I want out of my life, because I know that it is a horrible sin in God's sight.

Do you realise what doubt is? It is saying to God, 'You don't mean what you say.' Put bluntly, doubting the Word of God is saying 'God, you are a liar!' Said like that I'm sure that you, like me, want nothing at all to do with doubt. In fact the Bible says *'Let God be true but every man a liar.'* (Romans 3:4).

We need to face up to the challenge of the Word of God. There are no 'ifs' and 'buts;' He says *'they will lay hands on the sick and they will recover.'* (Mark 16:18) God didn't say that they might recover, or that they could recover. He did not say there is a chance they might get better, or that you might get a little bit of relief and improvement. The challenge we must face is that God said they will lay hands on the sick and they will recover. Now if God says that, who are you going to believe?

We are dealing with a question of authority here. It is why Jesus said: *'Heal the sick who are there, and say to them, "The kingdom of God has come near to you."'* (Luke 10:9). When you talk about the Kingdom of God you are talking about the government of God. You are dealing with the authority of God.

In Matthew 8 we read of the centurion who came to Jesus; His servant was seriously ill at home. Immediately Jesus said, *'I will go and heal him,'* which does say something about His eagerness to heal people. The centurion said, *'Lord, I am not worthy that You should come under my roof. But only speak a word, and my servant will be healed. For I also am a man under authority, having soldiers under me. And I say to this one, "Go," and he goes; and to another, "Come," and he comes; and to my servant, "Do this," and he does it.'* (Matthew 8:8–9).

The centurion recognised that Jesus was a man with authority, which astonished Jesus. Most of the people around Him did not comprehend who He was, or what He was doing. The centurion saw that Jesus had authority over sickness and disease and over every opposing power. He knew from his own experience, that if Jesus spoke the word of authority, that disease would have to obey Him.

Do you see the truth that the centurion saw? The centurion gave orders 'in the name of Caesar' and they were obeyed. He knew that because of the obedience he saw, Jesus spoke with authority. Today, as a man under Jesus' authority, I can speak with His authority. I can speak to disease and sickness in Jesus name and it has to do as it is told. Note that in Roman times certain names were more than titles. To speak in the name of Caesar was to speak with his authority, and if you disobeyed it was Caesar you were disobeying. A name could convey an understanding of the character and authority of a person, and so when we use Jesus' name, know that His character and authority are involved.

When Jesus gave His disciples their last instructions before ascending to the Father's right hand, He made this line of authority clear: *'All authority has been given to Me in heaven and on earth. Go therefore and make disciples of all the nations, baptizing them in the name of the Father and of the Son and of the Holy Spirit.'* (Matthew 28:18–19).

Jesus Christ is the same yesterday, today and for ever. (Hebrews 13:8). He has not changed and all authority is still His. Accepting that is the key to receiving your healing, today. If Jesus walked into the room where you are now, in His

114

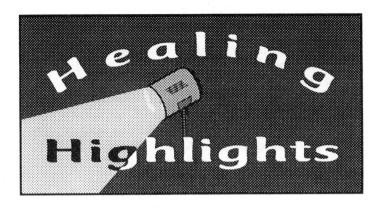

Neville Williams

School teacher Neville Williams contracted an infection in his left ear, whilst on holiday in 1963. He was treated by doctors but the infection soon spread and eventually he insisted on seeing a specialist. The consultant's diagnosis was that Neville's eardrum was damaged beyond repair. He was able to cure the infection but the eardrum had been very badly scarred and distorted. Neville was left with only 5% hearing in his left ear and nothing could be done to change that.

On holiday in 1984, Neville and his wife visited Malvern to see friends who were at the Good News Crusade's Family camp. Neville and his wife decided to stay on for the evening meeting. During this meeting there was an invitation for people who were deaf in the left ear to go forward for prayer. Neville went forward and was prayed for by one of the team.

Nothing seemed to happen! Neville went back to his wife and she whispered in his ear to see if the prayer had worked. To his surprise he found that he could hear her voice very clearly. Since then Neville has found that his hearing loss had been reduced so that instead of losing 95% of sound, he can now hear 95% of the sound around him and the improvement has been permanent.

physical body, would you have any problms asking Him to heal you? Of course, the answer is No. But, the truth, the reality is that He is here, present with you now. Read to the end of Matthew 28 and there is the proof; Jesus has promised to never leave you.

'But without faith it is impossible to please Him, for he who comes to God must believe that He is, and that He is a rewarder of those who diligently seek Him.' (Hebrews 11:6). It takes a step of faith, to accept the truth of the things we are discussing. But, a key to this kind of faith is to realise that faith is a relationship with the Lord Jesus Christ. It is becoming intimate with Him. As we hear Him speak to us, hearing the word of God, faith will grow in our hearts. (Romans 10:17). Jesus never fails, He always rewards those who diligently seek Him.

To end this chapter, let me share with you the testimony of Gladys (not her real name.) Her story illustrates what it really means to have faith in the Cross:

Gladys had a large, ugly goitre growing on her neck. *'By His stripes you were healed'* was the scripture focused on, as she was prayed for. Gladys went home with the goitre still there, but she went declaring that, 'By His stripes I am healed.' The next day she said, 'Lord, thank you for healing me, because by your stripes I am healed.' This went on for about a week; when she met friends who would ask how she was, Gladys would reply, 'By His stripes I am healed.' Her friends looked at her neck and did not believe her.

At the end of the second week it got so that when people said 'How are you today?' and she would say, 'By His stripes I am healed,' they would then say, 'But how are you *really*?' She could only say, '*Really*, by His stripes I am healed.'

Was Gladys being honest? Yes, because what God says is the reality. Honesty is saying what God says, not what you feel. Now, notice that Gladys didn't say, 'I am healed,' because that would not be honest; it is not true to say 'I am healed,' if you still have symptoms. However, the Word says 'By His stripes we were healed,' and to confess the Word of God is very different.

Gladys got into the third week, still confessing and believing, but still with the goitre very evident. One day in her daily devotional time with the Lord she prayed a unique prayer: 'Lord, I am so thrilled that by your stripes I am healed; I really appreciate you healing me Lord. But Lord, just for the sake of other people who won't believe it, will you take it away, please.' As she said that she went to touch the goitre – and it was gone. She received her healing three weeks before seeing the evidence, but she still received it.

Gladys is an excellent example for us. Faith without Jesus, without His friendship, is an empty shell; it's mind over matter. A close, living friendship with the Son of God enables us to believe and receive the truth. What a release from trying to do it by our own efforts.

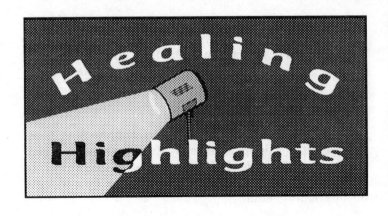

Mike Bettaney

'In 1973 I was a foreman on a building site in Prestatyn, North Wales. One day whilst testing a large diameter plastic pipe for leaks using compressed air, it exploded.

We had been given the wrong information as to the pressure required and were working at pressures four times greater than was safe. The pipe exploded about nine inches behind where I was sitting on the pipe and I was blasted up in the air and on to a concrete driveway.

I received many injuries which included severe cuts all down my back caused by shrapnel, two vertebrate were pushed in and another two were broken. I was taken to hospital and put on traction to try and reposition the dislodged bones and free the sciatic nerve which had become trapped.

Obviously the pain was immense. My surgeon told me what was needed to put me right. I needed an operation to remove the two damaged vertebrate; they would then take two pieces out of my hips and make new vertebrate from them and weld the new and surrounding vertebrate together. The surgeon did add that there were possible side effects. There was a slight chance that I would be paralysed, if the central nerve was damaged and there was also a bigger risk that I would be made sterile by the operation.

I was not prepared to take any of these chances and subsequently discharged myself from the hospital. I was in constant pain, my back would "give way" on occasions, causing me to collapse. I was on about 16 tablets of valium a day for the pain.

In 1977 Don Double came to Rhyl to hold a Good News Crusade Mission. I knew that I was going to be healed. I went along to the meeting with my wife and began to enter into the worship. Half way through the meeting as I was standing singing, I suddenly realized I was healed. No-one had prayed for or laid hands on me.

I have had no trouble since that time; it was a complete healing. Until fairly recently I was a weightlifting coach, and have also built three churches. To God be all the glory for the great things He has done.'

Chapter 11

Jesus is All You Need

Whenever I go to take a healing service, and especially when I am going to teach about healing, I feel very inadequate. Why? Because I know there are people who will be listening intently to every word I say; and however careful I am in the words I use, they will feel that I am making promises about the healing they so desperately want. I know I can't fulfil their desires, because I am not a healer. If I could heal, I would certainly heal everyone who came for ministry, on the spot. As I have said before, the truth is that I can't heal a fly with a headache!

Only the Lord Jesus Christ, the Son of God, is the healer and He is all you need. I can't heal anybody, but I have seen thousands of people, around the world, supernaturally healed. All healed by the power, and in the name of the Lord Jesus Christ. As we come to the end of this book I want to turn your eyes right away from man and turn them to the person of the Lord Jesus Christ.

He wants us to be spiritually whole; by that I mean that He wants us to know God. Knowing about God is not the same thing; it's like saying you know Princess Diana. However much you read about her, study the papers, even go to the places she visits, you can only know about her. To really know her, would mean becoming her friend, spending time with her. The same principle is true about knowing God. Many people know a lot about God. They have spent a lifetime going to

121

church, doing things they thought would please him, but they have never got to know Him in a real way.

> *'And this is eternal life, that they may know You, the only true God, and Jesus Christ whom You have sent.'*
>
> (John 17:3)
>
> *'And we know that the Son of God has come and has given us an understanding, that we may know Him who is true; and we are in Him who is true, in His Son Jesus Christ. This is the true God and eternal life.'* (1 John 5:20)

It is sad that so many people know so much about God, but they do not really know Him. Even sadder is that they think that what they are doing, week after week, will help them get into heaven. What do I mean? Well, confirmation, baptism, and church membership are of no value when you get to the gates of heaven. You can read the Bible from cover to cover, and know all the history of the scriptures, even take a degree in theology and still go to hell. What is necessary is to know the author, to know the God of the Bible.

It does not make any difference if you come from a 'Christian' family. Your parents and grand parents may be Christians, but that makes no difference to you. Every person needs a personal encounter with Jesus Christ, for themselves. Do you know God? Nobody else can answer for you, do you know God?

If you are unsure, if you can't answer with a definite yes, let me ask two further questions. Are you forgiven? Forgiveness is essential, you cannot get into heaven unless you are forgiven of every sin you have ever committed. To get that forgiveness means confessing your sinful state to God and then allowing the blood of Jesus to clean it away. As we accept forgiveness, the Kingdom of God has come near to us. Which brings me to the second important question.

Where is the government of God in your life? To put that another way, who controls your life? As a follower of Christ, His authority has to be a reality in your life. Do you choose what you do, and when and where to do it, or is Jesus in control? If He is, then it will not just be for a few hours on Sunday. I am talking about His control and direction 24 hours a day, 7 days a week, 52 weeks a year.

If you need to change your answers to these questions from No to Yes, turn to the end of Chapter 2 again, where there is a prayer that will help you make the change.

'For he who lacks these things is shortsighted, even to blindness, and has forgotten that he was purged from his old sins.' (2 Peter 1:9)

That word purged isn't an 'in' word in the Church today. That is sad because there is an important difference between being forgiven of your sins and being purged of your sins. The word has a radical connotation; it means that you go to the root of the problem, and don't just 'lop off' the branches.

Let me illustrate: You have committed adultery and come to God to ask Him to forgive you. You confess your sin, believing that His blood has cleansed you and so receive complete forgiveness. There is no doubt that you can be forgiven of any sin, including adultery, by coming to God as I have described. But there is a problem; what do you do now? The truth is that sooner or later you could commit the same sin again.

What is needed is for that sin to be purged. A purging is very simple, it is allowing the power of the cross of Jesus Christ, the power of the Gospel to get to work in your heart. Another way of putting it is to get the fear of the Lord active in your heart.

Let us bring it down to a simple level, because not everybody has committed adultery. I guarantee there is not one person reading this book who has not told a lie. The Bible says that all liars shall have their place in the lake of fire. (Revelation 21:8). In other words, every liar will go to hell. That is what the scripture says. You might think the ones you told are not counted because they were white lies, but they are black in God's eyes.

There is only one cure for telling a lie: come to the Lord and ask Him to cleanse you in His blood, as you confess it and ask

Him to forgive you. But as I have said, forgiveness is not enough, if you are not able to stop telling lies. Why is that? If we have only dealt with the symptoms and have not got to the root, the tree will continue to bear fruit.

'The heart is deceitful above all things, and desperately wicked; Who can know it?' (Jeremiah 17:9). The cross of Jesus and the power of the Gospel are the only things that can deal with a wicked heart. That is real purging, and it changes us from the inside. Every believer in Christ is a new creature, old things have passed away and all things have become new. (2 Corinthians 5:17). *'Then I will give them one heart, and I will put a new spirit within them, and take the stony heart out of their flesh, and give them a heart of flesh; that they may walk in My statutes and keep My judgments and do them; and they shall be My people, and I will be their God.'* (Ezekiel 11:19–20). That describes a true Christian.

In 2 Peter 1:9, it talks of a man forgetting he was purged. Now, I am sure you would agree that everybody forgets things. But, this is one thing which we can never afford to forget. Never forget what the Lord Jesus Christ did for you on the Cross, when He shed His blood. If you are a follower of Jesus Christ the things that happened to Him on the Cross, in the tomb, and as He rose from the dead, changed your life and need to be kept central in all you do. You can never afford to forget the power of the Gospel of Jesus Christ. The Bible calls those that forget Backsliders.

Not forgetting does not mean that you have to walk around all day saying, 'The Lord Jesus died on the Cross for me.' Rather the moment something goes wrong you are praying to Him to deal with it, and when something goes right you are praising Him for it. If you meet someone who does not know the Lord Jesus, you want to tell them about Him. You live constantly aware of the presence of Almighty God.

If that is not your lifestyle then it is likely that you have backslidden. My definition of a backslider is, 'someone who can remember a time when they loved Jesus more than they do, right now.' If you can remember a time when you loved the Lord more than you do now, you are backslidden.

Matthew Mulvenna

Over twenty years ago Matthew Mulvenna was serving in the British Army. One day, training on an assault course he slipped and broke his left ankle. Arthritis developed about two years later and Matthew was classed as unfit for frontline duty, and so lost the chance of further promotion.

The accident had happened because Matthew had been wearing plimsolls rather than boots. He blamed his P.T. instructor for not ensuring that he was wearing the proper footwear and for his loss of career.

At an Easter Conference Don gave the opportunity for anyone who was suffering from arthritis to be prayed for. As Matthew responded and went forward for prayer the Lord reminded him about his unforgiveness to the instructor. Matthew immediately repented and asked God to forgive him. At that moment he felt a heat in his ankle and he knew that the Lord had healed the arthritis.

Perhaps you are a Yo-Yo Christian. Sometimes up and in fellowship with Jesus, but sometimes down. Often a backslider will live like that, battling with a tremendous guilt; if that describes you, be encouraged, God wants to heal your backsliding. (Jeremiah 3:22; Hosea 14:4). Repent and return to the open arms of your heavenly Father.

God wants men and women who are going to join His mighty army and make a stand for Him. He is looking for people who are not just full of good intentions, but, people prepared to dare everything for His Kingdom; people with a back bone, not a wish bone. We are to be people of stability and that means we need to be whole people, whole in body, soul and spirit. God wants to heal us from every single thing that causes us to function at a level less than He created us for. He wants you healthy.

In this book we have looked at all kinds of healing, at the principles of faith and the rules God has given for healthy living. You have read many testimonies of those who have been wonderfully and supernaturally healed. After more than thirty years of involvement in the healing ministry, I am more convinced than ever that God will not be conformed to our methods. Some of the best documented miracles of healing are evidence of the Lord choosing to do things in a different way.

If you are prepared to believe for healing the Jesus way be ready for those surprises. Recently I was talking to the owner of the garage where I bought my car. I had witnessed to this man several times over the years. In the middle of our conversation about cars he said, 'The other day a man was buying a car from me and we got talking about religion. I mentioned you and what you do. He said that he had heard of you as well, and he mentioned what happened to his wife. She has had a very troublesome, gland condition for some years. She went to one of your meetings, where you had put your hand on her head and prayed. On the way home she felt all funny, but since then she has had no further problems!'

This had happened some time ago, and the man added, 'we are not believers, we are not Christians.' What God was, and is doing in that couple's lives I don't know, but I know He is doing it His way, and the result will be good.

I once met a lady who was in the last stages of Multiple Sclerosis. She had been taken around the country and all those who had any reputation for a healing ministry had prayed for her with no obvious results. One day the Lord walked into the room where she was lying bedridden, no one else was present, and He completely healed her. She got straight out of bed, and went to her piano and played for the first time for many years. What a testimony of God's grace; since then she has travelled to many parts of the world telling others of God's complete healing power.

For everything in life there is only one thing we need – the Lord Jesus Christ. If you need healing, then all you need is healing the Jesus way. If you have your health, give your life completely to Him, and go and tell others that they can be healed the **Jesus Way**.